off the map

CRIMETHINC. LETTERS / OLYMPIA / 2003

published by the CrimethInc. Ex-Workers' Collective
Additional copies of this book can be had for $3, including postage
costs. In addition to this book, we have also left a fair number of other
breadcrumbs behind us on our path into the dark woods: books, zines,
movies, music and newspapers are among them, some available from us for
free and others for a bit more. Precise coordinates and recollections can be
found at **www.crimethinc.com**, or for those wary of cyberia, try writing to:

  CrimethInc. Dreamers Union
  PO Box 1963
  Olympia WA 98507-1963

this is the second title in the CrimethInc. Letters series . . .
These are our letters—to the universe. To each other. This is where we re-
write our histories and create our own cultures without the mediation of
corporations. When we are too far away from one another for campfire
storytelling, we use our own voices here, to call out across the distance.

*Zine dissected and lovingly put back together again by scott to make this book
for two of the sweetest peas in the pod, whom he loves quite strongly.*

*Cover artwork by nikki mcclure, who cut the image out of a single piece of black
paper with an x-acto knife.*

Printed on recycled paper in Canada by the workers at Hignell Book Printing.

coordinates

preamble

We wrote *Off the Map* while we were living in a flat on the edge of the woods in Prague. The zine was our daily anchor; some days it seemed like we only emerged long enough to walk Ida, the golden retriever with whom we shared the flat, along with Didi, our mystic roommate who forbade us to cook with garlic, decorated the house with pictures of her guru Baba Ram, and suggested that excessive coffee consumption blocked access to the higher chakras. She moved out long before we finished the zine, taking Ida with her and removing our main excuse for leaving the flat.

When we first decided to write a zine about that summer of travel, we wanted to tell the stories that had shaped us so definitively, to give thanks for all the hands that had guided us along the way, to lend a taste of the wings we'd borrowed to anyone who might be waiting on the ground for an extra push. When we finally finished, after almost two months of mining our collective memories and trying to hammer it all into some kind of shape, we were so sick of looking at the thing that actually distributing it seemed anticlimactic. We agreed to circulate twenty-five copies a piece and let the universe have its way with them. And it did.

By the time we got back to the States, CrimethInc. had started distributing *Off the Map* in blurry, hard-to-read second-generation scammed photocopy form, purely as a labor of love. It worked well enough for a while, especially with all the help we got from strangers with access to copiers; but as free copies have gotten harder and harder to come by, and the demand for the zine hasn't let up, it was time for a change. After at least ten thousand copies had been copied and sent out for free by CrimethInc. and other delightful people, we decided that if *Off the Map* was to live on, it would have to be in the form of a book.

For some of us, zines are more accessible, more inviting; they tempt the reader to tell her own stories, to see that the author (or authors) are no heroines, no experts, but just people, just kids telling it like they see it, and live it. At this point, there are enough copies of *Off the Map* (the zine) circulating in the underground library that we trust they'll continue to find their way into the right hands. And let's face it, this book is a lot easier to read than that crappy dog-eared copy of the zine that's been read fifteen times—and you can finally see what the pictures are.

The urge to edit is almost irresistible. We can't see anymore with the same eyes that took in these stories, or speak with those voices; since these stories took place we've lived through exhilarating heartbreaks, devastating transformations, long stretches of brutal confusion and entire seasons of bliss, and it's tempting to tweak the old versions a little, to trim the bits that now seem excessively simplistic or ridiculously earnest and bring them in line with our more weathered hearts. But we haven't, because underneath it all, we still trust that vision of hope and possibility that fueled the writing of the zine.

We still believe in the viability of dreams, in and through and around the stuff of daily living, and even as the bedrock for our most solid practicalities. Dreaming is a dangerous proposition; it dares us to risk everything, to walk blind into the hills, to do the hardest work in ourselves and in the world—and to reap the richest reward. Sometimes, possibly, our dreams urge us to reveal ourselves intimately to an audience of strangers, and hope they'll meet us where we most want to be.

Yours in stories,

hib & xika

dedication

this is for all of the people who love us
and make us strong. for all of the people
who open their homes and their stories to
us. for all of the people resisting systems
of oppression. this is for all revolutionaries
and dreamers, big and small.

off the map

This is what it means to be an adventurer in our day: to give up creature comforts of the mind, to realize possibilities of imagination. Because everything around us says no you cannot do this, you cannot live without that, nothing is useful unless it's in service to money, to gain, to stability.

The adventurer gives in to tides of chaos, trusts the world to support her — and in doing so turns her back on the fear and obedience she has been taught. She rejects the indoctrination of impossibility.

My adventure is a struggle for freedom.

✭ ✭ ✭ more like spells ✭ ✭ ✭

The good thing about plane rides is that, if you're trying to get off clock time, it isn't that hard. You pretty much fly straight out of it. When you land on the ground again, your body and the clock completely disagree, and if you happen to have flown into a city you know nothing about, in a country that is not yours, with nowhere to stay and next to no money . . . well, there's really no reason to reconcile yourself with the clock. The clock becomes irrelevant, and Neptunian Time—the unclockable hours of sleeping or waking dreaming—takes over.

Hibickina and I woke up in a nettle patch our first morning in Europe, having successfully kicked the clock. The nature of our cheap tickets was that we'd spent a lengthy period of hell in airports. Once we touched down in the Netherlands, we spent another lengthy period taking ill-informed rides on trams that seemed headed towards Amsterdam. We were banking on finding a squat there, where we'd recuperate and get our bearings. Instead we spent the day swimming salmonlike in the endless stream of tourists that flood the city's center, following graffiti and staring hopefully at boarded-up windows to no avail. When evening closed in, we used the last of our energies for a drooping fire show. Two drunken Roman girls who were considerably less droopy lavished us with superlative praise, the fire was so amazing! *Where* had we learned!?! *Where* were we from!?! Not relishing the thought of associating ourselves with the hordes of

American guidebook tourists, we adopted thick accents and told them we were sheep farmers from Estonia. They were astounded that we spoke English so well. Considering how long it had been since we'd slept, so were we. They gave us their last guilders and Hibickina and I collapsed our weary shepherding bodies in a park at the edge of the city.

We woke to herds of business people speeding by on old cruisers, pedaling into the world of work. They were completely oblivious to the two sleepy women peering out at them from behind the screen of nettles and fir trees. After spying on them for a while, envying their bikes but not their destinations, Hibickina and I took the tram back into the city to continue our quest for a squat. We also had a new, more pressing pursuit: coffee.

Verottu Krottu materialized before the coffee. We were stumbling blearily down unfamiliar streets when I noticed a big inflatable black spider hanging outside a dusty window. It swung lazily next to a chipped mannequin leg, a rearview mirror, and a tiny pirate flag. Down below, every inch of the plywood that sealed off the building was wheat-pasted with flyers for squatters' meetings.

I eyed the door. It was spraypainted anarchist red. Passion red, I thought, or maybe a red carpet. Either way, a clue in the treasure hunt Hibickina and I were making of our lives. I knocked.

Nothing happened for a long while. I tried the bell, and finally a scrappy looking woman with a shaved head opened the door, standing pale and sleepy in the shadowy recesses of the hallway. A big black mutt was almost invisible beside her.

Yes, we could stay there for a night or two; there was even a room we could have to ourselves. The woman motioned for us to follow her up the stairs.

The stairway was dim and winding, with small, narrow wooden steps. What little light there had been disappeared when the door closed behind us, and we followed the woman up two creaking flights of darkness. The dog thumped ahead of us all, slipping past a wall of thick velvet fabric at the top of the landing.

"That's Guar," the woman informed us, pulling aside the velvet.

Immediately a gauzy light reappeared, revealing the fabric as an old wine-colored theatre curtain. Guar was already sitting in the middle of the living room, alternately looking pleased with himself and ferociously scratching his butt. There were more squatting flyers on the living room walls, and all sorts of resistance posters, recognizable by symbols but written in indecipherable Dutch. Streaks of filmy sunlight came in through the same dusty window we'd seen from the street below, and a mangy young calico lay where they pooled, purring contentedly to herself. A fake spiderweb hung above some healthy-looking plants, which grew eye to eye with a vine blooming on the other side of the glass.

"I'm Annet," the woman said, blinking through sleep-coated lashes and adding unnecessarily, "Ahhhm . . . I just woke up."

We introduced ourselves and apologized for having woken her, but she shrugged it off; squatters' hours, Neptunian time, don't worry.

"I needed to get up anyway," she yawned, watching Guar sink his teeth into the wiry hair on his backside.

We all just gazed silently for a moment; and then Hibickina sat down in a big old rocking chair, and I sat down on a silver spraypainted stool, and Minky the mangy calico crawled up into Hibickina's lap and Guar sidled up to me and rested his chin on my knee. A sweet sleepy comfort lay over the room. Hibickina and I had left home trusting that doors would open for us, but we hadn't imagined that what lay behind them would feel this familiar.

"Ahhhm, would you like some coffee?" Annet asked, brightening visibly at her own suggestion. Her pillow-lined face seemed to smooth itself out at the thought. We said yes in fervent unison, exchanging glances that said *well, we're definitely in the right place.*

"So," Annet surmised as she started brewing the coffee, "you are traveling?"

"Yeah." Hibickina and I looked at each other. How to explain? "Kind of."

We took turns narrating: we'd flown into Amsterdam yesterday on one-way tickets and dreams, but this was more than just summer traveling. We were both en route to lives we'd dreamed about. Hibickina was moving to Prague in the fall, and I would go there with her and stay for a couple of months before I moved to Barcelona. We would take our time getting to eastern Europe, check out Barcelona along the way, spend a month on the road together. We didn't exactly have it mapped out, and in fact, we didn't have a map at all. Our goal was to prove to ourselves that it was possible to make our dreams happen on our own terms, without using other peoples' maps, or money, or clocks. Or at least using less of those things, reshaping them so that they looked less like formulas and more like spells.

"Witches," Hibickina and I whispered happily to each other, looking around while Annet was in her room throwing on her fishnets and lacing up her combat boots, *"Witches living as they like."*

When she returned Hibickina asked Annet about the squat, and she said it was an all-female household, "except Guar," who looked up at her lovingly when she said his name. In English, Verottu Krottu meant something like *the ruin*, impossible to translate accurately but spoken affectionately in both languages. It had been squatted for two years. Annet caught the look of surprise that crossed our faces.

"Two years, it's not so unusual here. Some squats are shut down right away, or after a couple months, but some also last a long time. It's getting worse all the time, though, like everywhere I guess. More cops, more busts. Did you see the meeting flyers downstairs?"

We nodded.

"We're pretty organized. Once a month about 30 or 40 people meet to go squat a new site. It's fairly routine by now, we've got the tools for breaking the door and changing the locks, and we always choose the building beforehand. We usually meet at a park and wait until we have enough bodies to outnumber the cops. When our group is big there's not too much hassle. You know about squatting regulations here?"

Nope.

"Well, according to Dutch law, if a building's gone empty for one year, and people squat it—as long as they have a bed, a chair, and a table somewhere inside—the squat is legal and the squatters have rights. Of course it's not legal to actually break the door down, and if they manage to stop you from entering, you don't have any rights. But we're good at entering, and we bring the furniture right away, so as soon as we're in, we're in. You can walk right down to the city and register. Once a squat is legal, the building owner has to go through the courts and prove that they have some kind of plans for the building before the squatters can get evicted. But even that takes a while, a few months sometimes, 'cause first you have to get served a notice, and, well, you know. Systems." Annet grinned, the gotta-love-em smirk of someone versed in slipping through the back doors of capitalism to make some minor adjustments.

Another woman appeared on the landing from behind the velvet stage curtain and eyed us quizzically. She wore a miniskirt and several pairs of socks and black acrobat shoes, and as Annet left, Lucy introduced herself.

She'd lived at Verottu Krottu for a year and a half, Lucy told us. She'd been squatting off and on for over ten years, her longest residence a legal squat in Rotterdam, where the squatters fought constantly to keep their illegal garden space. The garden had been in an unused lot, and eventually, the law won out and it got paved over. After watching rows of carefully tended carrots, trellised tomatoes and nodding sunflowers drown in a sea of asphalt, Lucy left.

"I was tired of always fighting the police," she told us. "I wasn't strong enough to keep doing it . . . I needed some time for myself."

But by the end of the night I was pretty sure that Lucy was strong enough to do anything. She offered to take us to some of the good spots for fire shows, and when dusk settled, the three of us went out and walked the narrow streets. It was less crowded than in the daytime, and without the pulse of tourists pressing down on us, I had time to notice the cobblestones and the flower boxes, the stoops with their little pots of herbs and skinny saplings. Shutters framed almost every window, and the lines of the brick buildings curved with a softness I wasn't used to seeing in the States.

Everything was in bloom and, even beneath the bridges, reflected light formed flickering blue and white flowers in the dark waters of the canals. After Venice, Amsterdam has more waterways than anywhere else in Europe, and the notorious bewitching powers of that other city were understandable as we walked by rows of houseboats, gentle floating villages with gardens on their roofs and nothing to do but sway beneath the swath of starry sky. Easy to bewitch when you are living as you like, lost from the busier streets of life and found slipping quietly along a more meandering path. Below us I heard the slow shush of a paddle pulling through night waters.

Lucy walked ahead with lithe steps, a strong back and straight shoulders. Just watching her move felt good. Her acrobat shoes weren't for show; she performed with some other people and was involved with a circus freeschool. She looked like a warrior leading us, her fire stick spearlike in her hand, her body cutting through the myth of age limits.

"People say you're at your body's best at 25," she'd told me earlier, "that after that, your body only gets weaker. But I'm always getting better at acrobatics, and I'm stronger now at 36 than I was at 25. I didn't even start learning them until I was 24."

"I kinda want to learn some stuff about movement," I confessed to her.

"Keep dancing," she returned.

Later we all danced with fire on a crowded bridge while a wiry street musician played limbo music on his guitar, and my heart kicked the same beat as the knots of heat spinning past my ears, and I looked over at Hibickina moving snake-like through the orange light, and watched Lucy's strong arms twirl the flaming spear, and thought again: *witches.* Even after the police came and broke up our performance, and we were walking away with our chains still cooling, wrapped around our wrists, I could feel that power rekindling inside me. Less like formulas, more like spells.

amsterdam.

3 august.

life cracks open with just a little
tap, pours sweet milky sap right
down your throat. Learn to read
the signs and you'll find yourself right
where you need to be, another world
open at your feet. This is the place
we've been looking for since we were
small girls chasing fairies in the garden,
high schoolers in scowls and witchy black
clothes, angry young women who want
to get out, out, out of the systems we
hate & learn to shape our own lives.

This is a doorway, this beautiful
ruined house with its facade of
vines & mirrors, and the world behind
it has a thousand faces. Faces like
the women who have lived here in
Verottu Krottu for two years now, in
spite of the cops & the courts & the
steady encroachment of developers.
Lucy walking like a warrior through
cobbled streets. Annet slouched against
the counter at the squatters pub,
snorting with laughter, 'i'm not gonna
work, not me.' Micah leaning suddenly
out a broken attic window, one arm
around her scrawny cat and one
reaching out to toss the keys to us
in the street below.

Sometimes this not-quite-secret
world makes itself impossible to
ignore; it's like the brilliant dragon
mural painted four stories high and
100 colors bright, leaping out from a
squatted building in the heart of
Amsterdam. It's asking you — where
can we go when we let go of what
binds us? what do you want most in
the world, in this world of the possible?

 Kidnapped

Peter kidnapped us from a desolate interchange outside Utrecht. We were actually more interested in the waving fields of corn than in getting anywhere; he flagged us down as we walked past his car on the shoulder.

"This is a shit place for rides. I didn't even stop for you, actually, I stopped for him." He pointed to a skinny kid with messy white-blond dreads, who waved happily at us from the front seat, barely visible under the mountain of his pack and bedroll.

"I passed him two hours ago, then I got a flat tire and came back for him just now. So," he concluded as he packed our bags into his trunk, "it would be rather stupid to wait that long yourselves."

We soon discovered that Peter described everything as either "stupid" or "not stupid." He was chronically morose, asked lots of questions but seemed as bored by our answers as he was by everything else in the world—until he discovered that I knew about his favorite band, The Residents, a freaky underground carnivalesque troupe from San Francisco. He glowed as he raved about them; compared to the Residents all other music was . . . stupid. Peter was charming, in his own melancholy way, and since we were in no hurry to be in Paris by nightfall we followed him back to his house to meet his roommates.

The house turned out to be a small palace, a reincarnated Catholic hospital with cathedral-high ceilings and stained-glass windows. At the front door we were greeted by a life-size statue of a day-glo green bear in a top hat; paintings and sculptures dotted the walls and a row of damaged glass heads lined the staircase. The place was a cynic's version of Wonderland, the rabbit's hole squatted by four postmodern intellectuals on acid. There were only four people living there, which meant that all the Things in the house also got their own rooms: a room for the laundry lines, a room for a single desk and some paint jars, a room with nothing but photos covering one wall, a room for the two small rats in their refrigerator-sized cage, a locked room for Peter's enormous collection of bizarre Residents memorabilia and one for all the empty boxes it had been shipped in.

"The house, it's not so bad," Peter shrugged as he led us back in from a terrace that overlooked the entire town of Waaldwijt.

Before long, his roommate Ruud appeared, a balding and wiry distillation of joy.

"Ahh, hello guests! We will have dinner!" he cried as soon as we'd been introduced. "You look like maybe you don't eat meat? A meal with no animals, then!"

Ruud was Peter's antithesis. Everything was deeply fascinating to him; he sang constantly as he stalked energetically around the kitchen, interrogating us and nodding slowly as we answered, offering fragments of his own stories in response.

"All languages are songs," he explained tearily over chopped onions. "I learned Italian because each night I fell asleep listening to the flow, and in the morning I couldn't help but wake up and sing it."

We grew drunk on the liquid light of afternoon-into-evening, laughing steadily. With the intimacy of loving strangers, we pulled apart pieces of our lives and held them up for one another. After much goading, Peter modeled the long dress he'd sewn for himself and we crowed in admiration while he blushed proudly and stared at his Converse. Ruud talked about the silent madness that had filled him after too many years of travel and not enough of letting go. By the time dinner was over we'd plunged into politics and Ruud was making us coffee.

"I look around me and all I see is fear, a whole society built out of fear. But, you know, the world isn't just out there, it's in here." He touched his chest gently. "We have to make a space for ourselves." Words of encouragement crooned to recently hatched birds. *Go on, you can fly, you can fly, the wind is there waiting to catch you.*

We slept that night in the room with the laundry lines, strings of fresh clothes hanging over us like everyday banners. In the morning, Peter left us to pick up the road again from a rest stop crowded with cranky vacationers. Entire families gawked as they rolled past us, but who cared, we were already becoming practiced in taking as much space as we needed to stretch our wings. We stood between the road and a rustling birch forest, dripping with sunshine, singing unabashedly till finally we were scooped back into the rhythm of the highway, headed south.

too much glass

Over the guardrail, beyond a stretch of dirty grass and on the far side of the street, was a black graffitied squat symbol. Either by coincidence or by the whims of our old treasure hunt map, Hibickina and I had just been dropped off at a random bend in the freeway, directly across from a huge squat. We crossed the road to check it out.

We were snickering at all the posters for hardcore bands with names like *Carnal Rot* and *Infectious Dis-Ease* when the door opened. Three SHARPS came out, a kaleidoscope of spikes and camouflage and leather. They marched by us in a silent line. We stared after them for a moment, silent ourselves, before bursting into laughter.

"Punk scenes . . ." said Hibickina.

"Punk scenes," I said.

We were really curious about the squat, though, because it appeared to take up an entire block. From the outside it looked like enough room for a very small village, but only a row of ramshackle sheds and a cluster of boarded-up two-story buildings were visible behind the high surrounding wall.

As Hibickina and I were speculating, the door opened again. A man and a woman stepped out of the building. The

man assessed us briefly and started down the street but the woman held open the door and smiled.

"Would you like to go in?" she asked. "You can have some coffee, and maybe it will be a nice time for you."

We thanked her and entered the gloomy, cobwebby bowels of the building.

"If we do live in a treasure hunt," Hibickina whispered, "the clue is definitely coffee."

"Let's hope," I whispered back.

We followed a shaft of light out into the courtyard. It was just as big as it had looked from the outside. There were scraggly-leafed trees lining the edges, and some rockwork where gardens must've once been, but mostly there was bare dirt with lots of dog shit and dug-up holes. Still, it enchanted me because its latent potential was glaringly obvious. It *was* big enough for a small village, big enough for sizable gardens, for concerts and community space, big enough for a freeschool and a lot of living space. For a moment I imagined pear trees and grape vines and sweet peas, hammocks and swings, junk sculptures and bikes. Even in its neglected state, it was easy to have an affection for the space, not only because it was full of possibility but also because it was claimed. Because it had been taken back from the land of forbidden shipwrecked buildings and put into the hands of half grown-up kids, who had just enough dreams and just little enough money to make their fort out of its ruins.

We ventured around one of the inner walls and peered down a long alley to a table where two girls were sitting. A convoy of madly barking canines ran to greet us, and one of the girls called out, "Hey, do you want some coffee?"

The dogs escorted us down to the table, where the girl introduced herself as Kimmi. A tuft of green hair poked out from beneath her backwards baseball cap, and she had the usual bunch of piercings, and myriad bracelets, ripped black clothes and big boots. But her eyes were huge and frog green, wreathed in thick lashes, and her face was washed in rich chestnut freckles, and the end effect was that she looked more like a lovely elf than a scrappy punk. She brought the coffee, carefully moving aside a pile of fuzzy pink fabric scraps that looked like fur.

"Were you here for the show last night?" she asked.

"No," I explained, "we're actually hitchhiking to southern France and somehow we got dropped off right across the street from here, and we were curious about what you all were doing with the space."

"We have all these ideas about reclaimed space and making community, but our own ideas can only take us so far," Hibickina added. "It helps to see what other people are doing."

"We're not much of a community here," Kimmi sighed. She reached for the two small kittens who were stumbling around under the table and scooped them up gently. They fell happily into her lap, purring loudly as she kneaded their bony bodies and pulled fleas from their soft new fur.

"I mean we have these shows but that's about all we do together."

The complex was home to nine people and eight dogs. There was a common kitchen and living room in the main area, but Kimmi said they were filthy, so she and her boyfriend lived together in this wing. I looked around. It was pretty filthy too. Kimmi was the brightest thing there by far. She squished another flea, examining its flattened body on the tip of her thumbnail.

"I just *can't* get rid of them," she said bleakly, shaking her head. "The dogs have them too, and I think they might have worms. They need a special diet."

The dogs thumped their tails on the concrete floor, nudged her ankles. She reached down and scratched their ears, sighing again. Apparently the dogs hadn't had it easy. Kimmi had rescued them from a bad situation knowing they deserved something better, but she wasn't able to give them all she wanted to. And the constant looming threat of eviction only added to her worries.

Belgium, she explained, had similar squatting regulations as the Netherlands, but in practice the police here operated more like cops in the States, storming places without any notice, routinely taking violence to extremes. It was riskiest when the squat held big concerts like the one last night, she added, because it attracted attention to the place. But so far their squat had survived, and they'd managed to keep putting on shows, although they weren't as good as the shows in St. Brieuc, at the train squat . . .

Train squat?

Yeah, she said, it was wonderful; this old train station was squatted legally. The police had actually been the ones to tell the squatters the place was empty, and encouraged them to take it, so it would draw squatters away from the center of town. Since it worked out for both sides the squatters didn't get hassled. And Le Wagon was really organized; it held shows that people came from all over Europe to see, and the squat was so cool . . . Kimmi's gestures grew lively as she described it, her pale hands caught the sun and little pieces of kitten fur drifted down from her fingers. The shows happened in the station building, she said, and there were still boxcars on the tracks, which had each been made into individual bedrooms for the squatters. They had a garden.

Wow, what did you say the name of that town was? St. Brieuc? Hibickina wrote it down.

Kimmi took us upstairs so we could see the room she shared with her boyfriend. I followed her up the shallow steps, not expecting it to be any different from the rest of the halfhearted household. If the people who lived there didn't really talk to each other, it was hard to imagine big creative projects happening anywhere in the squat, the way it sounded like things did at Le Wagon.

We emerged in a dim room. I almost tripped over two huge stuffed dog beds sewn from the same fabric that had been on the table. Two very fluffy, very pink creative projects.

"I made them," Kimmi announced shyly.

"They're beautiful," I said. They were.

Above an unused fireplace, rows of little glass jars held

brown herbs. Others hung in loose bunches and Kimmi fingered their dry leaves.

"These are for my boyfriend," she explained, "because sometimes his feet are very smelly, and this helps them."

We went downstairs just as the stinky-footed boyfriend returned with two of his friends. They were the SHARPS we'd seen outside the buildings earlier, and they emoted nothing more now than they had then. I wondered if we needed badges before we could get in the scene, or if there was just no hope for us since we were female. Stinky Foot showed Kimmi a propane tank he'd gotten so she could use the stove.

Watching the exchange unfold, I was thinking cynically, *oh goody, man hunts down stove so woman can cook.* But Kimmi had something completely different in mind. "Oh, good!" she exclaimed, "Now I can cook for the dogs!"

It turned out that the SHARPS and some of their other friends were heading out to a party near Lille, which was on our route. Somehow Kimmi convinced them to give us a ride, and they finally turned to us and sort of grunted an acknowledgement, so we said goodbye to Kimmi and followed them back out through the pitted yard to their van. Once we were underway, the van got so full of carbon monoxide fumes that we put bandanas over our faces for the duration of the ride. It seemed kind of extreme but so were the fumes, and it certainly wasn't like we were missing out on a great conversation. The SHARPS were pounding beers in preparation for the party, smoking joints with the same grim silence of their original exodus. I wondered if I had misunderstood, and they were actually en route to a funeral. The only time anyone said anything was when they stopped to pick up more hitchhikers, two young Swedes who took one look at our quasi-balaclavas and asked, "Are you anarchists?"

On the way to Lille, I sat in the back of the van feeling carsick and staring out the window over my bandana. The whole scene with Kimmi had made me kind of sad. The squat was organized enough to hold their bi-monthly shows, but not enough to function as a community. The boys were experimental enough to dress punk, but not enough to challenge gender roles. And Kimmi was just trying to live her life in the middle of it all.

"Too much glass," she'd said when we asked about gardens in the squat. But the way her voice was full of defeat, and her eyes far away, she could've been talking about anything.

chariot of deliverance

Was Paris just a nightmare? Had we really navigated the trams of hell last night? Were we still trapped in the city's gridded suburban outskirts? Let me marinate in my dreams a moment longer. . . I peeled open a sticky eye. Nope, I hadn't made it up, here my grimy grey body lay stiff and fully clothed in a nest of blackberries. My sleeping bag was padded by wild grass and weeds, sheltered from any outside observation by the briars and the remains of a vine-eaten brick wall. It was an overgrown pocket in the tamed slacks of suburbia. It was a fertile womb on the edge of a sterile desert. Ok, I thought, peeling open the other eye and deciding on a good mood, it was damn cozy.

But it was still suburbia, and worse yet, early Sunday morning. Our stomachs were shrunken from the day before and growled feeding orders at us, but nothing was open. Nary a patisserie in sight and all we had was Dutch change anyway. We walked toward the onramp, banking on a quick ride to the next town where we would somehow get a chewy loaf of fresh French bread. I could almost taste it, and even though my muscles were knotted, and my teeth were furry, my spirits were high. I thought of Christophe, the sweet man who had picked us up an hour before Paris yesterday, and taken us directly to the public transit station so we wouldn't get stuck trying to hitch through the city. I thought: I believe in people. It's not the mystical benevolence of god that I count on day-to-day, it's the goodness of other human beings, the kindnesses lying ready in the human heart. I believe in the goodness of people and people bring me goodness. It was with this wash of gratitude that I stuck out my faithful thumb on the A-10.

It wasn't exactly a high traffic area. Every five minutes a carload of churchgoers sped by in their Sunday best. My mood had put a big dopey grin on my face, which I directed outwards at my fellow humans, the goodness of whom I fully trusted we would soon be graced with.

Unfortunately most of these humans were more interested in gracing god than in gracing us, and their worship-bound minivans with rows of empty pew-like seats had a funny way of speeding up when they saw us standing there on the shoulder. After a while the shoulder began to seem more like an armpit. My faith was wilting.

Our destiny was finally altered by a kind man on the end of a poodle's leash. We all followed the poodle across town to a place where, the man promised, we would hit more traffic. At the top of an embankment he left us with a smile, and we followed his directions down a scabby path. He hadn't been kidding. There certainly was more traffic, and it was all coming toward us faster than the devil. There must've been some misunderstanding about us actually wanting someone to stop for us. But if god's people wouldn't stop at the other spot, and satan's people couldn't stop here, how the fuck would we ever get to our French bread?

There must've been some black magic afoot because all of the sudden a car appeared. From nowhere. Neither of us had seen it come and neither of us saw it stop. It was just there, dark and gleaming, the chariot of deliverance.

We looked at each other uncertainly. Was this really possible? Maybe it was only a phantom. Should we get in it? A gorgeous dark-skinned man with sunglasses and the poise of Lucifer stuck his head out the window, did we want the ride? Hell yeah, we were hungry.

We were headed for the south of France, and as it turned out Richard and Sabram were going all the way to Spain. Richard was Italian, and Sabram was French, and in Spanish they told us the tale of how they met on a beach. At first we thought theirs was a love story with a twist, but later Sabram spun an alternate version in which he too had been hitchhiking, and all our deductions flew out the window. If they were driving a car that could materialize out of nothing, we figured, there was no telling where they themselves had come from.

Almost immediately Richard pulled over at one of France's roadside mini-villes, the full service refueling centers that provide the freeway traveler with the opportunity to perpetually avoid the rest of the world. Hotels, gift shops, gas stations and restaurants all built in a glittering array of garish neon. Every voyager's need anticipated and provided for in plastic glory. "Are you hungry?" Richard asked, parking near a café made mostly of plexiglass. He didn't wait for an answer, of course we were, so was he, that's why he'd stopped, he bought us French bread and coffee, he did everything very quickly, would we like chocolate?

Back on the freeway we were separated from Richard and Sabram by a 700 decibel wall of music, which made conversation impossible, but we were joined with them by a chronic plume of smoke as they made their way through six successive packs of Marlboros, which made breathing impossible. Luckily for our lungs Richard stopped every half hour to get more coffee and to buy us more food, bananas and dried apricots, dark chocolate. He had a thick leather wallet that matched the plush interior of the car and it seemed to be standard practice for him to sugardaddy his passengers, no expectations. We kept an extra close eye on the road signs just to make sure we remained headed in the right direction, and France was getting left in the dust at an alarming speed. The other cars on the freeway were one long blur as we flew down the fast lane. The entire day seemed to be moving at an ever-increasing pace, and Richard and Sabram were talking more and more rapidly to each other in the front seat, and gnawing on the ends of their cigarettes, and what was that they were taking with their eleventh shots of espresso?

Oh dear. Speed.

They made a detour to take us to our destination, telling us they were on their way to some seriously good partying, why else would you go to Spain, here was the number to Richard's cell phone which Sabram had been answering all day (what the hell was their relationship?), we should join them, all expenses paid, party party party . . .

In a cloud of turbo speed exhaust they left us standing dizzy and nauseated in the tiny deserted center of the first real town we'd seen all day, disappearing as quickly as they'd arrived six hours earlier. As the dust settled we ripped up the number they'd given us, and searched our pockets for Liliane's.

down like honey

Liliane came to pick us up, asked us how our travels were, looked us over and casually mentioned that she had both a shower and a washing machine. She looked maybe sixty, quiet face, strong arms, bronzed skin, the gold flash of a mended tooth. When she laughed it came out hesitant and surprised, like she herself wasn't expecting it. But she didn't laugh much, she paid attention to the road, two hands on the wheel, fifteen kilometers of pine-lined asphalt, then a sharp turn into Moulin Vieux.

In exchange for room and board, WOOFers (Willing Workers On Organic Farms) can work at family farms or other small enterprises. If squats are the urban solution to traveling broke, WOOFing is the rural solution. Liliane's bed and breakfast had been listed in my old xeroxed WOOFing guide, with a description of her organic garden and an intriguing reference to caravan accomodations.

I was sitting in the back seat dreaming of deserts and camels as we jounced down the last three kilometers of rutted sand. We passed a stately two-story farmhouse which Liliane

nodded at—"that's it"—and a few hundred yards later we lurched to a stop in front of a half-sized green trailer, resting its weight unevenly against the weedy ground.

"So, here is your caravan," Liliane announced, showing us into a stuffy interior layered with months of summer dust and spiders. The floor was dry rotting, and seedy curtains were pulled over blighted windows with cracking rubber seals. It was a squat in the woods. No majestically draped tapestries and not a camel in sight.

Up in the farmhouse tub I rinsed rivers of grey off me, grey and more grey, until the current swirling down the drain finally ran clean again. My fresh skin felt unfamiliar to me, and Hibickina's face looked markedly different out from under its cloak of grime.

In my new state of cleanliness I tiptoed around the quiet house. Liliane's son was an artist, and he'd done most of the renovation, sculpting flowers and the faces of goddesses into the desert-colored walls. Each room was carefully tended; nothing was out of place, and even the shadows seemed arranged in the early twilight. The curtains hung long and loose, white lace in all the bedrooms, billowing white cotton in the kitchen, reams of dark maroon fabric hanging on chunky rings in the living room. Our caravan might be reminiscent of the squats we actually stayed in, but not these spacious rooms. It felt like a palace.

Panes of bare glass still held the heat of the day in the solarium, but the large kitchen was cool in the gathering dusk. The scent of summer rose up through the open windows from the loamy garden soil below. Liliane had laid a meal on the long hardwood table, shallots and garden salad, quinoa and sheep cheese, olives and wine.

"I think WOOFers like to drink a lot of wine," she said prophetically, filling our glasses.

"Oh, we're not much for drinking," we told her truthfully, memories of a drunken Amsterdam still rocking in our minds. We recalled wasted tourists laughing shrilly to each other under neon lights, drunk frat boys with thick wallets at little cafes, drunk girls with clown make-up laughing at their stupid jokes; drunk punks at squats, punks headed to other squats to get drunk. Ugly drunks and mindless drunks and boring drunks, and not really any drunks that inspired us to join them. And now here was Liliane offering to fill our glasses with velvet-thick Bordeaux local.

It went down like honey and we spent the next week drunk in the evenings. Moulin Vieux's main meal was dinner, so after we'd made up the rooms in the morning and picked at the weeds in the garden for a while, we had free time until we were transformed into waitresses at night. Liliane was a kitchen witch, calling buttery vegetables and thick spicy patties out of the oven, making magic with steamy rice dishes, organic bread, cauldrons of fruity desserts. We dug out the long skirts we'd kept rolled up in the bottom of our packs in case we'd need disguises, and wore them slung low over our hips, enjoying the freedom of being obviously female. Road travel was a life away. The thin loose cotton swung easily against our bare thighs, supposedly dinner clothes to keep up with the bourgeois guests but it felt like the fabric of Jezebel to us. Everything was sensual. Our bare feet slapped softly across the kitchen tile as we carried platters of Liliane's fragrant spells to the outside table where we all took our meals together. We were toys for the guests, our stories a fun game in French; where had we come from? They interrupted Hibickina's careful French to answer for us although she was perfectly capable of finding words of her own. It didn't matter to them, they were on vacation, they poured us more wine. They poured themselves more wine, told the same dirty jokes every night, laughed uproariously every time.

We slid in and out of the high farmhouse doorway, transforming the table from one course to the next, our bodies gliding smoothly on the heady waters of that velvet-thick Bordeaux local as we delivered spreads of gourmet cheese on grapeleafed platters. We winked at each other across the cloth isle of stains and laughter, silently watching the stars creep out over the darkening ridge of spiky pine trees. We rolled our eyes at each other when our paths crossed in the kitchen, and afterwards, when the table was empty and the guests had climbed the shining wide-planked stairs to their seashell-colored rooms, we washed their mountains of dishes and gossiped in giddy giggling whispers. We felt like maids in a castle, more like girls than women, more like nymphs than girls.

The waxing moon greeted us after our work, smiling down on our round drunken bellies and secret bare thighs. The creaking garden gate closed one world behind us and the cool moonlit paths opened another.

In the afternoons we walked along the sandy tracks that wound through the pines, our callused feet scuffing the silky surface into low rhythmic shrieks, our conversation lazy and wayward. We traced patterns in our memories, we daydreamed, we thought we could follow the sand all the way to the ocean. But hills broke into more hills and later Liliane told us the sea was fifty kilometers away.

On our walks we collected small treasures for the altar we had made in our caravan: acorn cradles, miniature blossoms, bits of old rusted iron. The woods were sparse, like those in faerie books, with shafts of sunlight falling in perfect lines between the trees. A creek caught petals of light on its surface, spun them, tempted me into its shallow icy waters. I curled up and let them swallow me completely, then lay naked and gasping on the scratchy grass trying to convince Hibickina to make the same venture.

"It's worth it," I promised, watching prisms of water slide off my eyelashes onto patches of dusty earth. There were ants bustling around where they fell, and hungry mosquitoes were taking our bare asses as an invitation, and I hadn't tasted summer like this for years. Liliane had a treefort in the back yard, cobwebby bicycles to loan us, and 200 yards of swing-strung zip line.

Sometimes we were demure and dreamy women bracing baskets of clean wet laundry on our skirted hips, pinning pillowcases to the line to dry in the hot fragrant wind, but mostly we were laughing kids playing witch in the familiar folds of summer.

Late in the week, the air hung in still sheets, oppressively hot but golden. All day we sat around drinking coffee and eating bread and honey and talking about how bored we were in the cool of the kitchen. Then we laughed at ourselves because we knew that when we told our stories later, we would forget that we were ever bored in these regal rambling rooms in the southern countryside of France.

Liliane was gone to the beach, having instructed us that it was too hot to work, and no guests were there so we had the house to ourselves. When we got tired of the kitchen we went into the piano room and lay on the rough woolen rugs, still moaning happily about how bored we were.

After a solitary dinner of garden vegetables and wine, Hibickina and I set off down the sandy tracks of the driveway for our customary moonlit walk. The air was like bathwater, still, quiet and warm. As we walked along, staring up at the stars and the opal of the nearly full moon and watching for the meteor shower that was supposed to happen. Hibickina pointed out Persius.

"Is he some character from Greek mythology?" I asked her.

"Yeah," Hibickina said. "He killed Medusa."

I'd been thinking a lot about Medusa lately, feeling a kind of kinship with her, and hearing that ole Persius had killed her, I automatically didn't like him and I said so to Hibickina.

"Well, she was turning people to stone and all," Hibickina said. "I think Perseus was rescuing some babe."

We continued along, our limbs loose from wine, the scent of pine fresh in our nostrils. I considered Medusa. I'd never studied her, but even so, something didn't sit right in me with her story.

"I don't think it's that she actually turned people to stone," I finally said to Hibickina. "I think that's just a metaphor for their fear. That when they saw such a real, such a wild, magic and powerful woman who lived so unapologetically outside the confines of domesticated femininity, well

. . . they were forced to face their own fears about what that meant. Which probably rendered them as immobile as stone, mentally or physically."

"Hmmm," said Hibickina, watching for meteors. Her tangled curls made a halo of snakes in the shadows.

After a while, we found a stride, even with the difference in the lengths of our legs, and walked easily down the country road together. I looked over at her, face pale in the moonlight, already transforming the world around her into poetry that I would get to hear later. Then I turned my own face back to the sky, winking at the moon, watching for the meteor shower, which never came. But the shooting stars were just as good, and I made wishes on every one.

The noon-high sun held a quality of eternity as we hitchhiked out the web of quiet country lanes from Moulin Vieux, and it seemed like August had paused just for us. The black asphalt was so bright it looked wet, the trees were leafed with brilliant emeralds, the roadside dust lay rich and tawny. I felt confident in the world, pleased with myself and my traveling companion and our place off the map, pleased with the hot lush day drenched in technicolor. I could tell that things were gonna come easy to us this day.

We got dropped off across from a cornfield, so I stole into its leafy corridors to get us some lunch. Hibickina's laugh rang out over the valley when I reemerged, sheepishly crossing the road with big yellow ears sticking out at all angles from my overalls. It was a difficult situation in which to be sneaky, but the corn was sweet and fresh and we were back in scrapping mode.

When a little red car approached I winked at Hibickina. "Here's our ride." Sure enough, the driver stopped, hopped out and started opening up the doors, falling all over himself in a way that suggested falling was his usual manner. He was around our age, with an eyebrow barbell and a pointy chin piercing, long eyelashes and full lips. I raised my own eyebrow at Hibickina, and she winked back at me as she climbed in.

Julien was a drummer in a hardcore punk/skate band ("You like? Skate music?" he asked, throwing up his hand in Ozzy Osbourne's infamous gesture and rasping, *"Skatecore!!"*) Our chauffeur was driving home to the little town where he worked in a corn factory. He tried to explain his job first in English, then in French, and finally I figured it out in Spanish. He wrapped labels around cans. When he wasn't informing the world of the contents of canned corn, he toured Mexico and southern California with his band. He kept switching back and forth between French and English and nonverbal charades, but he was so bad at communicating, it seemed like he must have no first language at all. He kept all three of us laughing hard, though, shaking his head at himself, sticking his tongue out, smiling wide and charming us.

The mystery of his linguistic shortcomings was solved when he pulled over almost immediately to roll himself a joint. "You want? Ecstasy?" he offered, and we said no thanks, and soon we were back on the road playing charades.

We were sweeping through the south of France toward the city of my dreams, zooming down velvet green country roads with an adorable French punk boy who was flipping off the too-slow cars and yelling *"Merde! Merde!"* every three seconds, and my good feeling about the day wasn't wearing off. I rolled Julien's cigarette so he could stay concentrated on the cheerful yelling, and the sticky strings of tobacco meshed into a cylinder of summer between my callused fingers. The gum on the paper was sweet and tacky when I licked it closed. I lit it. The cherry burned the ripest color of sun.

Hibickina and I looked at each other with easy wordless understanding when we saw mysterious things on the horizon, or when abandoned buildings caught our attention, or when we knew we were both thinking the same thing about

Julien. Her open-sky eyes were all lit up, her apple cheeks were glowing, and each time I turned around to face the front again I got a straight shot of contentment to be sharing the road with her. I was used to traveling alone, responding to the world completely internally, which sometimes made me feel like an island. Now we were two on the island, and the island was a lot of fun that way, and really more like a boat. A boat navigating by shooting stars, avoiding Persius, and headed for the sunny shores of Barcelona.

Jean-Pierre eyed our packs with a nostalgic smile as we climbed up into the roomy cab of his truck, sighed dreamily and said, "I spent forty years out there. Forty years on the road." He glanced at the rearview, like he was making sure his past was still there, but all it caught was a ribbon of asphalt snaking out over industrial France.

I was curious about what could end forty years of tramping, but he didn't offer much of an explanation, just said that a decade back he'd needed some money, so he started driving trucks. He shifted the gears slow and steady, and I imagined him making the transition from shoulder to driver's seat in the same manner. His eyes were gentle and pale blue. They reminded me of the worn glass from broken bottles that washes up on the shore, the kind of bottles that once drifted over the face of the sea with blurry messages printed neatly on damp paper and sealed carefully behind their corks. Bottles which had been shattered on unexpected sharp rocks, their fragments softened by water and time, their messages undelivered. His eyes held forty years of all those beginnings, once upon a times which had never quite reached the shores of happily ever after.

He asked us question after question, where were we from? Where were we headed? What were our zodiac signs—a

Capricorn, he laughingly guessed, a Pisces. Had we traveled before now, and had we noticed the waxing of the crescent moon last night? He was thirsty for our tales of wayfaring. No more sleeping in cornfields for Jean-Pierre. Now it was just petrol stations and the radio. Tracy Chapman's *Crossroads* was playing, and he started telling us about how he used to travel with a left-handed guitar and a repertoire of original French blues. We all sang along over the buzz of the speakers and the rumble of the engine. *You'd sell your soul just to keep your shell / I'm tryna protect what I keep inside / all the reasons why I live my life . . .*

I wondered if Jean-Pierre ever used his CB radio. If the truckers ever talked to each other about their personal lives, or if his colleagues had any idea that a wanderlust dreamer was at the helm of this roadbound 18-wheeled vessel, with 40 years of adventure stories in his wake. I wondered if anybody ever asked where he came from. *I'm tryna protect what I keep inside . . .*

When Jean-Pierre dropped us off at the edge of the next city, his eyes misted. "Picking you up has been the joy of my day," he said, and we thanked him for his kindness and stood on the sidewalk waving goodbye as the oversized semi tires bumped back down to the asphalt. He had a delivery to make in fifteen minutes, and we had good tread on the soles of our shoes, and nowhere to be but the other side of town where the freeway picked back up. I watched Jean-Pierre shifting gears to realign with the flow of traffic, still waving at us, until we were nothing more than ghosts disappearing from the silver of his rearview.

Hibickina and I walked through Tarbes, talking about Jean-Pierre and all of the stories that sit untold in the hearts of older people. We're all fed such false messages about success in life, made to believe it's a point of arrival. So most of us spend our whole lives waiting to arrive. We expect that once we get there, the long story of the life we just lived will be infused with meaning. But while we're waiting our voices dry up. They forget how to ask, they forget how to listen, they forget how to tell.

We wandered down streets lined with patisseries and pharmacies and charcuteries, past a tiny hillside park veined with stone tunnels, and Hibickina sang me bits of Utah Phillips' song *All Used Up*.

"I spent my whole life making somebody rich / I busted my ass for that son-of-a-bitch / he left me to die like a dog in a ditch / he told me I'm all used up . . . He used up my labor / he used up my time / he plundered my body / then squandered my mind . . ."

I watched our feet skip over the cracks in the sidewalk out of old habit.

Hibickina sang to the rhythm of our steps: *"They use up the oil / they use up the trees / they use up the air and they use up the seas / but what about you, friend! and what about me . . . ? / what's left when we're all used up?"*

She paused, reaching for the last verse. *"Sometimes in my dreams I sit by a tree / and my life is a book of how things used to be / and the kids gather round and they listen to me / and they don't think I'm all used up . . ."* The song still hung in the air after she'd finished, and my chest tightened.

"That makes me so sad," I told her.

"Yeah," she said. "I think that most of us are always afraid that ultimately, we'll end up alone."

"I want something different," I said.

She looked over at me. "Me too. And sometimes I remember that that's what I'm working to create. That it's actually possible to always have people around me who know me and love me and grow with me."

As she was talking, I could feel it for a moment, what it would be like to live outside the fear of that ultimate loneliness, to be certain that you would partake of life the whole way through in the company of your most beloved friends. It felt amazing. It felt like clothesline sheets in July sunshine, light and bright, catching the cool of a breeze. I wanted desperately to create what Hibickina had just described in my own lifetime. Looking over at her, I knew I was on the right road.

Just then the road we were following wound past a series of individual garden plots and fruit trees which comprised a community garden and orchard. A shaded bike path bordered its rows of apple trees, and the scent of hard cider drifted up from where the fruit had fallen. It was right in the middle of town, a small island of life, producing carrots next door to business as usual. An old man was out tending some of the trees, filling rotten spots in their trunks with bark mortar. Not far beyond the gardens was an enormous junkyard, heaped stories high with rusted bed frames, old planks, the iron arms of factory machines, antique bicycles. At the very top was a dilapidated sailboat, sailing the small ocean of sunken but salvageable treasures. Hibickina and I stopped in unison, awed. The late afternoon light hit the hull at an angle and lay in rusty pools on its ancient deck. Rising up from its ruined body, the mast still pointed toward the sky.

We stood gazing at it, the sun warm on our own shoulders. The air almost seemed salty and I was elated by the triumphant journey of the small remembering boat, moored in stars and resilience. The old man stopped his work, braced a gloved hand against his brow to shield his eyes from the light. We waved at him and his thick fingers slowly left his face, drew a crescent in the air, returning our greeting.

On the far side of Tarbes, a tag artist had been at work. Funky Chunky Mazee was the signature, and through the French, we couldn't figure out if Funky was saying that graffiti was an art, so in these days when art is a crime, that makes even noble Picasso a beast . . . or if what she meant was actually long live graffiti, the true art, and fuck Picasso that pretentious art world asshole. Funky's second message was clearer: *Think for yourself . . . contest the authorities*, advised Funky. Hibickina and I concurred with our absent new friend. We were inspired to take the airbrushed ads on the wall behind us into our own inky tagging hands. But the work day had just let out, and there were too many people on the sidewalks, hurrying past each other in high heels and wrinkled slacks. I stood between the rows of glossy ads and the busy people who were inadvertently guarding them. Everyone looked tired or worried and I thought again about the force of fear connecting all of us.

When we peel back all the layers of pain and distrust and neurotic surface fears, what lies beneath is that infinite primal terror of being stuck forever with no love. We have built our societies on the pursuit of success: traditionally that's meant beauty for women and power for men, although increasingly these overlap. Daily, we see around us the dismissal of the ugly, the weak, the old, the powerless. So we know that one day it could and can and will be us who are dismissed. Whether we have the tools to fool everyone until we are old, or whether tomorrow someone sees our cracks and stains and rejects us, the fear of isolation is valid because all around us are images confirming that isolation is our destiny. Buy your way out of isolation, out of dismissal and anonymity, say the corporations. Try this product, this shampoo, this razor, this cellphone, this car . . . blah blah blah. Buy *in*. But the billboards of sexy girls gaining the attentions of powerful men are empty promises of reward when below them an old woman sits alone at a bus stop.

Corporations sell us tools to aid our division into leagues of power and beauty. But they lose customers when people start crossing the lines of their own volition. Often stories are the ways that lines get crossed. Stories enable us to imagine how it might feel, for a moment, to be the teller. They show us all the places where we overlap and help us understand the places where we don't. They offer us insight into other times and places, and through their intimacy, they make other worlds real. They show us that other worlds are possible.

Stories and streets are powerful venues for contradicting the imminent doom of loneliness. The public art we make of ourselves in the street, the languages of our bodies tracing postures and assuming them, the paths of our eyes grazing each other, are either participatory or resistant. Here, in public, we can choose to change our immediate world by remaking our myths and telling our own stories, by remembering how to ask and listen, and by learning to show our most real faces to each other and celebrating them. Show your warts, and you defy the very process of airbrushing the truth. Risk smiling at the person sitting next to you on the bus, and immediately the message of isolation is undermined. Not just for the two of you, but also for those watching this unusual event unfold. The moment we notice that we can make fresh choices every minute, the moment we take Funky's advice and think for ourselves, it's easy to see that we're all in this together. Isolation was somebody else's bad idea.

(revelations

Hibickina and I had been walking for several kilometers, halfheartedly scouting a place to sleep and wholeheartedly talking love and politics. The sky was suspended between violet and ebony when we found our spot, a patch of dewy grass beneath a massive oak tree where crickets were singing smooth electric songs and acorns kept the time by dropping onto our heads. The moon looked like abalone through the black webbing of leaves above us. I lay awake for a long time watching it set, and when I finally turned on my belly to fall asleep, I noticed tiny points of blue light forming a miniature constellation, which moved slowly through the dark wet grass. It was a glowbug, inching along the bridges the blades formed, humping itself over small hills of damp earth. Sometimes I lost sight of its luminescent migration; the fiery pinpricks momentarily disappeared in an abyss of shadow. My eyes tried to pull it back out, to reignite the darkness with its small bright journey, and when I didn't find it right away I started doubting that it had ever been there. But it always reappeared, teasing my flickering faith like a breath of wind. I vowed not to close my eyes until it had passed by, I vowed not to miss a moment of its magic, but when the thickening stars told me we were halfway to morning, the steady blinking pace of the glowbug was still in sight.

I realized, then, that the nature of magic is not passing by. Under the waning moon, everything was suddenly steeped in profound and mystic meaning. I was no mosquito-bitten traveler stealing past tattletale farm dogs to sleep in a borrowed field; no, I was a student of life's poetry, deep in the throes of epiphany. And the glowbug was an undercover philosophy teacher, reminding me that magic isn't something that only happens once in a while, when someone is really lucky. It's happening around us all the time, and if we look hard enough we can see it shining through almost anything, even if we have to squint. It's up to us if we stay awake watching it or fall asleep lulled by it. It's up to us to trust that it's real, and if we do, a whole world opens for us to live in, not in place of irritating dogs and hungry mosquitoes, but right alongside them and within them.

As I laid there staring at the ole glowbug I couldn't believe that I ever had moments of blindness to magic, let alone days and weeks and years. I was certain, in that late hour of contentment before I fell asleep in soggy socks and damp overalls, that the imprint of the glowbug would last forever, that never again would I live outside of such enchantment as was mine for the claiming. It was with the assurance of fresh revelations that I finally gave myself up to dreaming, the glowbug still inching over the ridges of my mind, in no hurry to reach the morning.

When morning came, we were covered in acorns and slugs, and I had yet another revelation. Dog shit was an unavoidable fact of life. The flies were already out, buzzing around impatiently while they waited for us to move our sleeping bags off of the crumbling piles so they could eat breakfast. We brushed off the stinky dried flakes, and had our own natural breakfast of nettle seeds, chickweed and elderberries before walking back out to the road. The dogs were docile by daylight, not even twitching their tails as we passed by. Perhaps we smelled more familiar to them this time.

outsiders

Our ride left us in Palamos with a reassurance that we'd be able to sleep in seclusion on the beach. We eyed the hotel and nearby high rises cynically, but we climbed out of the cab anyway—*muchas gracias*, good luck, good travels—and wandered toward the smell of the ocean. We walked past fields of tomatoes and late-season strawberries, incongruous amidst twenty-five story luxury condominiums still under construction. Hasty run-down shacks poked out between rows of greens and bright plastic piles of produce crates, and I wondered if the future residents of the condos would object to the constant presence of an unavoidable economics lesson in their front yard. A few blocks further we came at last to the beach front, or rather, what would have been a beach if it weren't covered by an endless string of hotels, restaurants, discos, bars, souvenir shops, and a dozen yards of concrete. You could still hear the ocean, though. Almost.

I sat waiting for my compañera to come back with food, leaning on our packs and watching the procession of clean faces like neatly made beds. I felt perfectly out of place, one small and very dirty creature obviously carrying everything I owned on my back. Obviously off the market. Every pair of eyes that wandered over me seemed to size, box, and label me in a single glance. To the nervous, smiling moms I must have been the worst possible thing their offspring could become; as they passed me they pulled tightly on the small hands that held their own. Younger kids looked at me uncertainly, like I might have been part of the circus . . . mysterious conjurer or horrible freak, it wasn't yet clear which.

I watched group after group of pre-pubescent girls wander by, most of them fifteen at the oldest, always the same skin-tight skirts over flat stomachs and undeveloped breasts, high heels, perfect make-up and shiny blonde brushed-for-hours hair. I imagined they'd been out trying to get into clubs, trying to put themselves on the market. Was that what passed for adventure in their world? There was an undeniable, nearly visible line dividing us, made out of money, out of social power, out of beauty; I was as displaced from their side as they were from mine.

When Kika came back to rescue me from the crowd, we fled immediately to the lip of the ocean, the only place where any sort of dark or stillness wasn't chased away by neon and a constant thumping bass rhythm. We'd been trapped in various vehicles all day, the blue Mediterranean just beyond our fingertips, and we couldn't wait anymore to swim, so in spite of all the practical reasons not to do it, we left our clothes on the rocks and slipped in to the water. The moon floated full and fat against the waves, washing the sickly neon pulse of the strand off our dirty skin. Two late night surf-fishers stood silhouetted out on a pier, their voices drifting slowly down the beach toward us. Farther away, a dark knot of boys passed the glowing cherry of a joint around their tight circle. Even so, as we rocked on the warm tide we could have been alone with the milky moon and the sand, a pair of tired mermaids whispering just for the sake of having secrets to keep.

Eventually our own fatigue drew us out of the water and back into our sweat-stiff clothes, both of us still tired and no cleaner than before our swim. As I shoved salty tangles of wet curls out of my eyes and hauled on my pack I wished silently for a simple, safe place to sleep. But what should have been a simple prayer turned out to be more like a self-inflicted curse.

We headed down the beach, hoping our secluded spot would soon magically appear, but the ocean was never separated from the strip of bars and buildings by more than a few feet of sand. We crossed back over the no-man's-land of the road, past the swank hotels and back the way we'd come through the fields, and nowhere, nowhere, nowhere was there a place for two exhausted and increasingly irritable former mermaids to throw down their packs for even a few hours. Finally we found ourselves in a quietish sort of neighborhood, and peered around hopefully only to discover that all the yards were surrounded by high gates and higher walls.

Resting her hand on the side of a parked pickup, Kika turned to me and snapped, "I'm just gonna sleep right here!" The truck's bed seemed barely deep enough to shelter her and was completely bathed in the sulphurous yellow glow of a street lamp, not to mention the fact that it was marked on the side with some company's logo, obviously a work vehicle, and the work day was only a few hours from dawning. I thought sullenly of all the mornings I'd struggled to coax Kika awake, trying to persuade her out of somebody's yard or business or private whatever before John Q. Propertyowner arrived to do the job for me.

"Kika," I said in a poor semblance of an even voice, "do you think you're going to wake up early enough in the morning so that we don't have to deal with some pissed off guy who's already had too much coffee and doesn't want two filthy girls in his truck?"

"Well I'm certainly not going to sleep in luxuriantly, am I?" she snarled.

I returned her evil look just as evilly.

"Fine!" I spat back. "Then I'm just gonna sleep on the ground where it's dark!" I threw my pack down huffily into what I would later realize was a writhing, active anthill.

As far as sleep goes, that night was arguably one of the worst of my life. The streetlights buzzed, the neighborhood dogs barked like clockwork and came sniffing around me and the truck. From an open window spilled the nasally laughter of a pack of drunken Spanish women, howling almost till dawn. Worst of all, my skin itched like it was on fire but I couldn't rouse myself enough to figure out why; I was dirty, sure, but I didn't have scabies yet. Finally, as the sun came up, I looked at my arms and legs, now covered in small but militant ants, and sighed from the center of my bones. I loathed this shit tourist town and I hated all the tourists, actually I hated Spain and I probably even hated traveling, I hated bugs and dogs and especially the awful women laughing all night. I hadn't yet decided whether or not I was going to hate Kika.

I stood and looked at her, scrunched in the corner of the dirty pickup bed. Her arm was pulled like a blanket over her eyes and her spiky porcupine hair stuck out in fifteen directions and her face was still streaked with salty grime in spite of our late night swim. I could tell she was trying desperately not to be awake, but she had the exact same saggy-eyed, I-hate-the-world-and-I-might-hate-you look I knew I was wearing. And I couldn't help myself—I took one look and I just started laughing, from deep in my sleep-deprived gut. Kika looked back for a few seconds, still bleary and on the edge of irate, before she started in too. We stood there while the sun bloomed pink and polluted over Palamos, laughing till we couldn't breathe. Laughing at the ants in my hopelessly snarled hair, at our pointless anger from the night before, at our grimygrey skin, at even the hideous hungover memory of the awful main strip. It was the same as the laugh of the up all night Spanish wolf women, howling at the improbable raucous mess of it all, till the sun comes up and you just have to start over again.

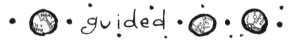

It was early in the day when we washed into Barcelona on a tide of hot dry air. With my heart still buoyed by recent kindnesses, I felt light enough to ignore the city's salient flaws: air too heavy to breathe, sky more brown than blue, blocky buildings and enormous signboards making it impossible to imagine the ocean just a few streets away. In other places, I told myself, Barcelona is full of Gaudi's dreamy buildings, and somewhere in this city is an airy yellow room that overlooks an open market, a life waiting for Kika to fill it with words.

We took the Metro into the center of town, toward Plaça Reial, where we'd easily be able to meet other squatters, or so we'd been told by a friend's friend. The metal mouth of the subway spit us onto La Rambla, a main touristy drag lined with street vendors and newspaper kiosks, the usual map and souvenir stands sidled up next to fast food stalls and pricey restaurants. The little islands of commerce that give structure to a sea of concrete and birdshit and meandering human bodies. Street performers were starting to appear as well: illustrators drawing on-the-spot portraits and actors posing as statues, so well-disguised we were startled when they opened stone-colored eyes.

The street was strangely full of birdsong; every few meters we passed a stall selling tiny finches housed in tiny wire cages. Stacks and stacks of wings rustling uselessly, feathers falling to the cement. We stopped and eyed one distracted pair of bird-sellers occupied by a small mob of young girls.

"Kika, how long do you think it might take to open all the doors? Hypothetically, that is. I'm just wondering."

"Well," she said slowly, "I think if all the cages happened to fall, if someone accidentally bumped into them, it might not be easy to tell just what was going on for a few minutes. Of course, I think anyone who knocked over all those cages might want to leave quickly."

She shifted her heavy pack meaningfully. We kept walking.

When we got to Plaça Reial, we realized immediately why our friend's friend had thought this would be a good place to find squatters and other punks. It was filthy, occupied by groups of kids in dirty black clothes, accompanied by herds of unhealthy dogs. Under the heat of the sun the whole place reeked of human piss and dog shit. A fountain hissed weakly in the center of the square, and in its pitiful patch of shade a sallow woman was trying to sleep with her head on her arms.

The police also seemed to think this was an excellent place to find punks and squatters and other undesirables and they cruised through on foot or in cars every two minutes or so. Eventually they pulled an armored paddywagon in to

block the main entrance, and fished through the assorted groups of misfits and vagrants until they found one to pull away, a skinny brown teenaged boy who spat *No sabes nada, nada!* as they shoved him along.

None of this seemed to deter the tourists, though. The plaça was lined with hotels and al fresco cafes and it must have been listed in some demented guidebook because groups of sightseers kept wandering in and staring beleaguredly around them, faces saying vacantly, is *this* the place? They looked at us the same way they looked at all the other human scenery, vague and detached or with latent hostility for ruining the composition of their snapshots. They took pictures of each other in front of the famous filthy fountain, bought ice creams and wandered out the same way they'd come in. I wondered how many vacation photo albums would later feature my scowling face somewhere on the "Afternoon in Barcelona . . ." page.

When we could no longer pretend there was shade left to hide in, we left in search of Espai Obiert, a radical cultural center we'd been told about back in San Francisco. We found it a few blocks away, an unobtrusive blue door in an unobtrusive brick wall, but a sign in Catalan and Spanish told us Open Space was closed. This seemed to be a hand-lettered distillation of Barcelona's essence: locked, shuttered, and unavailable, potential promise lurking off limits just behind a thin wall and we couldn't find the door.

We crossed back over the flesh and concrete river of La Rambla and into Barrio Gotico, the oldest part of the city. The streets grew narrower and narrower, wide arteries branching into veins, until they became a net of nearly indistinguishable alleyways. We walked for a few minutes, dulled by the roar of traffic and sticky August heat, lost in our heads, before we abruptly realized everything had changed. Gone were the looming signboards and graffitied fences, the blinding white sun flashing off glass and steel. Here, it was quieter. Hypnotic. Dangerous. The light filtered down through layers of wrought iron balustrades, balconies covered in vines and flowers and laundry that hung absolutely motionless in the afternoon heat. The air was almost eerily still, cool and shaded by tall stucco buildings that deadened the noise from the arterial streets. Something was out of place, though, something glaring but impossible to name . . . until I realized, birds again. The alleys were full of birdsong. Even in this poorest, dirtiest part of the city, where the streets are full of piss and the *plaças* reek of shit and the trash is piled halfway up the buildings, somehow people are trying to remember that creatures in cages still have wings and songs.

The streets never got washed in this part of town, and neither did the walls, which were covered in graffiti years thick. In other cities we'd been able to read the walls like a secret map, signs that told us where we could expect to find open doors. There were squatters' signs and anarchy symbols everywhere in Barcelona, but each time we explored a hopeful building, it was the same story: no answer, if we even found a door to knock on. Finally Kika approached a pair of local guys rummaging through a pile of broken furniture outside a building that looked suspiciously squatted. First in Spanish, then in English she asked them cautiously about the building and about other squats nearby. One of them shrugged us off and turned back to the crates and mattresses, but the other sized us up with black eyes brighter than anything else in the dingy street and finally said, "You look like you need some help, so I'm gonna help you." Apparently we didn't have a choice in the matter.

He turned and marched off down the street, tossing his words back over his shoulder in a swagger that almost kept pace with his feet. His name was Tito—it's Cuban, you know?—and his friend Opa had a squat with a garden he sat in all day, and we could for sure stay there, he'd just tell Opa we were old friends of his from before he came to Spain, only Tito couldn't quite remember where was the squat so we'd just find his other friend Jose who lived there and who he had to find anyway because he had Tito's fucking guitar, man, you know?

Our excitable guide led us to a triangular plaza which was, if possible, even filthier than Plaça Reial. It was filled with locals who eyed us cynically, though Tito seemed to know every third person in the square. Each time he talked to somebody new, Tito introduced us as friends looking for a squat. Invariably, the person we were talking to would eye our packs and look up at the sun, still a good three hours away from setting, before telling us solemnly and with genuine concern, you'd better get rid of your stuff soon, it's almost dark and this neighborhood, it's not so great at night. These were not tour guides warning the tourists to keep an eye out for pickpockets, these folks lived in the barrio. After the third or fourth successive warning, we began to grow a little concerned.

Tito, however, went on carelessly in his singsong English, spoken so rapidly it might as well have been Spanish for all I could understand. I caught just enough to figure out that no one seemed to know where Jose was and Opa hadn't come out of his garden for days, nobody knew any squats and no they hadn't seen his fucking guitar. Finally, a skinny girl with snaky dreads told us diffidently, oh I think it's maybe that way, you know, with a black door and a bell marked Tijuana. She pointed vaguely up an alley.

It didn't take us long to discover that nearly every door in Barrio Gotico appears to be black by virtue of dirt or age, although none of them have bells marked Tijuana. Clearly, Tito had no idea where he was going, and no plans to admit the fact. He talked incessantly; we asked him about Cuba and how he'd ended up here, and he threw back answers which frequently had little to do with the question and often trailed into song. *La bananita loca, se bane en chocolate . . .* By now we'd somehow been joined by several of Tito's friends, spiky blond-haired Courtney, who spoke Spanish with an outrageously bad American accent, and her silent girlfriend Maria who trailed along behind us as we trooped through the streets. I couldn't help thinking of the fairy tale where more and more villagers get stuck with their hands on the golden goose, winding helplessly through the town until someone finally frees them by cutting off the goose's head.

Suddenly Tito shouted, "This is it!" He seemed as surprised as we were. We had appeared abruptly before a high yellow wall spray-painted with the words *Okupat tu tambien!* "In Catalan that means, 'you squat it too,'" he explained paranthetically before he began yelling for his friends at the top of his lungs. He was like a schoolkid at show-and-tell, a pre-hormonal schoolkid hyped up on too much sugar. I was waiting for neighbors to appear and dump buckets of water on all five of us.

"Um, maybe we should look for the door," Kika suggested sagely.

Finally, after much pacing and peering and, on Tito's part, grumbling and shouting, it became clear that Opa and Jose were not likely to come out of the garden. At this point neighbors actually were beginning to appear and glare at us evilly. Tito threw up his hands dramatically and said, "Well, you stay with me tonight and we'll find them tomorrow." He charged off in a completely different way than we'd come, leaving us grinning behind him.

Later that night, after we'd settled into the dingy red and blue flat Tito shared with about nine hundred irritable Spanish men, and had a chance to explore the city a little on our own, we found Tito again at the corner bar. We talked for a while and he drew us a map to the beach, explaining it four or five times in detail and asking with concern, "Can you find it? I can show you the way if you need me to . . ." I cut him off with a smile.

"Tito, you are so good. Thank you for helping us this way."

He smiled back wider than the widest street in Barcelona and said, "Let me show you something." He turned to the wall and with his finger traced a capital A, drew a circle around it. He winked at me. "Get it?"

I wanted to kiss him but I just winked back. Got it.

• the making of the map •

The folks at Espai Obert looked surprised to see us again, like they hadn't believed that these two bumbling Americans could've possibly been serious about wanting specific directions to Barcelona's padlocked underground community. But we proudly produced a city map, and after exchanging a bemused glance, Judit and Ivan instructed us to lay it out on the table.

Slowly they walked us through the cracks: here was a squatted *centro social*, a cultural center for the resistance community. Here was a radical bookstore and info center, and over there, across town, was a huge squat with eleven years of history. Another *centro social*—lots of concerts at this one, they said—and see here, the local co-op. Soon the map was a constellation of carefully numbered red dots, and my journal was scrawled with the corresponding descriptions and metro directions . . . the city anew.

I tried to thank Judit and Ivan but I was getting sick. I felt like a slug with cotton in my ears, an underwater slug with oxygen deprivation and a thick tongue behind the bars of my teeth. My Spanish was getting worse by the minute and I wanted to leave before I further humiliated myself in front of these patient people who I hoped might one day be my friends. They hadn't been pretentious about peeling back the surface of the city and I'd skirted enough scenes to know that realness was a rare gift. I liked them a whole lot; I liked the way that they seemed to see past my bad Spanish and overly dilated pupils straight to my curious dreaming heart. I liked the way they took my not having the answers as me wanting to learn, not me being stupid. Their openness made me feel like maybe there would be a place for me in Barcelona after all. Maybe the honeyed moon we'd watched drip over the water last night would shine on places other than Barrio Gotico, other than Plaça Reial with its shutter-faced junkies, other than the teeming *ramblas* or the rows of polished storefront windows in the business section.

I hadn't thanked them enough and I had more questions, but my head was spinning. What was Judit saying?

"You can stay at my house, *si quieres*," she offered. Her voice was soft and clear, carefully enunciated so I would understand her better. "But it's not a squat."

"Oh, thank you," came my quick conditioned response. "That's a nice offer. I'm sure we'll figure something out."

It wasn't until Hibickina and I were back down on the sidewalk that Judit's invitation sunk in. The kindest woman we'd met in the city, who just happened to be a collective member of this amazing radical cultural center that we were both interested in, had opened her home to us, and I'd said . . . no?

It was a leftover reaction from a genteel custom where people said one thing and meant another, and made offers they expected you to refuse. But this wasn't genteel America, this was Spain, and I hadn't come all this way to politely close the door someone was offering to open for me.

I stood there staring at the sidewalk, trying to overcome the inertia of habit and impending sickness and make my leaden legs climb back up the seventeen miles of stairs. Eventually I found myself back in Espai Obert, stammering and blushing my way through an explanation that yes, we would very much like to stay at Judit's flat, after all. Without the thick cloak of words to hide behind that a native language easily provides, a sharp honesty is necessary, and equally so a faith that others are communicating exactly what they mean. It's too complicated to weave mazes of shy requests or equate thanks with guilt. So this time I just said thank you from the bottom of my heart and didn't question that, for whatever reason, Judit could see enough goodness shining through our dirty faces to trust us with her keys.

We hadn't exactly fallen through the cracks in Barcelona; instead we'd gotten a guided tour by generous revolutionaries smart enough to know that if you want the cracks to widen, sometimes you have to show people where they are. But as Hibickina and I trudged across town to the Keimada flat, winding through the metallic streets which lay like a suit of armor over the hot breast of Mediterranean soil, the city seemed to seal back up. I noticed face after face with eyes devoid of doorways, and building after building with barred windows. It was past siesta time and still everything was closed, carefully shuttered against both inquiry and intrusion. The open laughing streets I'd imagined were absent, the colorful expanses of free public space I'd dreamed of were turning out to be properties as private and guarded as the faces. Everywhere the message seemed to be one of fear: guard what's yours, and keep it under lock and key.

I didn't want to guard what was mine, I wanted to throw open my doors and give it its wings. I wanted to let it out and share it with the world. It had been locked up for too long, and Barcelona was the place I'd chosen to learn how to be my own boltcutters. Maybe it was a choice too arbitrary, maybe it was too much like an arranged marriage, but I wasn't giving up yet. Not when I'd just been handed keys and a map.

At the Keimada flat, we were immediately greeted by Luna, a thin black familiar who wound around our ankles in skittish spirals. We followed Luna and Judit's flat-mate Raquel down a long hallway to the kitchen, which was a homey configuration of dishes piled on the drain board, a table hand-painted with a sunrise of stars, and a refrigerator covered in posters for *luchas*. On the walls were a squat phone list, information about Espai Obert, and flyers for musical events. It looked more like our friends' homes in Olympia than anywhere else we'd been since we left, and I felt a wisp of homesickness wind up my stomach. The signs of punk politics were all around me, but the people who lived here were squatting their daily dreams, not just reclaiming buildings and forgetting to fill them up. They were engaged in struggle for a big revolution but they were also living it right in their own small kitchen. A comic about *ocupas* hung on the wall, a self-directed tease which caricatured squatters and implied an ability to notice all of the cliches, shortcomings, and ironies of the movement Keimada was part of, without abandoning it; an ability to not take themselves too seriously.

Raquel started making . . . yes, we were in the right place, according to our old treasure hunt map. Here was the clue.

"Do you want coffee?" came the familiar invitation. *Claro*, of course we want coffee, and maybe we will never want to leave this *casita milagrosa*.

All of the Keimada flatmates—later we met Dani, Nuri and Maite—were politically active, busy every day with meetings and jobs, parties and events that had them out late at night and up early in the morning. Constant laughter flowed through the bustling kitchen. It was the heart of their collective household, meals taken easily together, food cooked communally and paid for with an untracked honor system. The systems of organization all seemed organic and natural at Keimada: there were no exacting accounts kept, no chore charts, just an expectation that everyone would do their part, and everyone did.

In the mornings the women walked around half naked until they took their showers, sleepy-eyed and saggy-pantied and comfortable. Part of it was the heat, the sweat that was impossible to ever fully rinse off, but most of it was unselfconscious habit. They hung and folded laundry, washed dishes, made crepes and coffee, all with bare and imperfectly gorgeous bodies. Lived-in bodies, bodies claimed like favorite forts, bodies forgiven and broken-in and used like a well-loved pair of shoes. These bodies lived in nonchalant pleasure, outside the jurisdiction of magazine pages, housing the hearts of what I was certain must be *las mejores luchadoras* in the city.

The *Fiestas de Gracia* were happening during our stay in Barcelona, a seven day extravaganza of music and culture that stretched for blocks and blocks in the old Gracia neighborhood. It had once been a local event, a tradition in celebration of the barrio, but now most of the streets were filled with processed pop music, plastic decorations paid for with corporate money, and expensive confections. There were nightly alternative activities, though, and Hibickina and I decided to check out the less capitalistic face of the fiestas.

We wove our way through the throbbing crowd, snaked along the edge of a teeming plaza until we came to one of the *centros*. A long line of very drunk crusty punks, *los crostos*, was sitting on the curbside out front. Inside, the cozy nook of velvet couches, the shelves of worn books I'd imagined, turned out to be only more surly-faced kids buying cup after disposable plastic cup of warm beer. Nobody appeared to be having a very good time. Looking at them, I suddenly felt very far away from home. I missed my friends, whose politics were familiar to me, centered in love. What did I have in common with these kids except for some traveling scuz and a faith in anarchy? I searched the faces and the walls for something recognizable, but all I found were huge murals of cartoon death images. Hope doesn't always wear the same face, Kika, I told myself. Maybe its face is actually a skull here.

Death is a cultural shadow that often gets shoved under the rug, and examining it is important. But most of the time I find myself starving for life and creation, saturated with both internal destruction and the destruction happening in the outside world. It was only fitting that Hibickina and I were studying squats. Our entire lives have been squatted by systems we don't believe in, and our very souls have been occupied by indoctrinations which destroy our ability to love and create, and which take away our freedom from the inside out. It's time to squat back, we had agreed again and again, time to stake claim to the bones of human history and sew upon them new flesh. Maybe that was why the caricatures of skeletons were so prominent in squat culture.

But how did I want my world to look? I was tired of defining it by negatives: I don't want this, nah, not that for me . . . Hibickina and I had traveled an entire circuit of squats and named more of what we wanted to avoid than what we wanted to create. If we were going to define by negatives why were we bothering with alternative communities anyway? We might as well just head for corporate reality and hang out there.

Hibickina touched my arm lightly. "Kika."

I started, my half-rant reverie broken. "Yeah?"

"Do you want to go home?"

Home. I'd been lost in thought for ten minutes, immobilized by the seeming emptiness of a place where I didn't want to be. What I wanted was to try to get inside life, not stand in doorways, watching and judging from the peripheries, until one day I woke up old and realized that for all my stories, I didn't care that much about telling them. That meant I better choose the right doorways and go inside. And while Olympia was two continents and an ocean away, the Keimada flat was only a twenty minute walk from here, and we had keys.

"Yeah," I said. "Yeah, let's go home."

Kasa de la Muntanya is an anarchist fortress. A former outpost of the Guardia Civil, the Kasa looms over the hills of Gracia, rubbing dusty stucco shoulders with the world-famous Parc Guell. It's a bizarre juxtaposition. On the left, a chaotic black-flagged castle, complete with small towers, parapets, and an enormous oak door that could withstand a battering ram. Probably it already has. On the right, the public park that showcases Antonio Gaudi's fairy tale buildings, all tidy curves and glossy mosaic murals, alongside pricey cafes and souvenir shops. Parc Guell is one of the most famous spots in Barcelona; it's probably featured in every guide book from Spain to the North Pole, and it's usually populated with a herd of sightseers armed with several hundred video cameras. In the stairwell that separates the house from the park, someone has painted an impossible-to-ignore mural, a caricature of a camera-laden tourist with bulging eyes, fists dripping dollar signs. Beneath it, "Tourist, you are the terrorist!" in bright unhesitating letters. Its location puts the Kasa strangely in the limelight, a piece of the radical underground face-to-face with a glaring pocket of capitalized culture. Hard to say whether it's in spite of or because of this visibility that Kasa de la Muntanya has remained squatted for eleven years.

We spent an afternoon in the Kasa with Charlotte, a Dutch expatriate who'd lived in the Kasa for the past several months, and Uwe, who'd lived there almost since it was first squatted. They laughed seriously, constantly, chain-smoked hand-rolled cigarettes, and poured us endless cups of thick, dark coffee. As we repainted the doors and windows with sickly green oil paint, Charlotte told us about the time she'd helped organize a weekend conference for an anticapitalist group.

"We had to feed everyone who was coming, you know, so we thought we'd do kind of a 'stealing action,' you could say. We got the idea from some people in Paris. The plan was, a couple of people would go in and fill their pushcarts with food, and then the rest of us would make like a parade, a demonstration outside. At a certain time, they'd rush out and meet us and we'd all go off together, with the food. Only, I guess it worked better in France. Here, it was a disaster." She was already shaking with stifled laughter.

"Some people got stuck inside the market and the ones that got out had mostly grabbed bottles of expensive wine. Another group turned up to help us feed people, but it turned out they'd brought 50 kilos of meat with them—in their suitcases, I guess, and they'd come all the way from Paris! So there are all the vegans, practically taking up arms against the meat eaters—it was like civil war. Meanwhile the French cooks were completely *outraged* that there weren't enough tables and people had to sit on the floor. It was just the end of the world to them." She was trying to collect her breath enough to finish the story. "Oh god, it was really terrible. A weekend like that and you're almost ready to say okay, never mind, the capitalists are right!" This only sent all of us off into fresh gales of laughter.

Once we could all breathe again, Charlotte and Uwe gave us a tour around the enormous house, showed us up to the gardens on the roof of a nearby building, told us about the current project of installing a bathroom on the top floor of the house and their hopes for adding a solar oven. They grew serious as they explained the current situation with the squat: after a court case that had been dragging on for years in an attempt to remove them from the house, they now expected a final eviction notice within the next few months.

"We will resist, of course," Charlotte said, looking up at the gathering dusk.

At its core, the squatters' movement is always a story of resistance. Squatting invalidates the boundaries of private property and sets immediate human needs before arbitrary law. In doing so, it absolutely refuses two of the things which are essential to any functioning capitalist society. No wonder it's so quickly and forcefully squashed; creating new choices is usually fatal for the system they replace.

When I first became radicalized, I learned to say no: to authority, to oppression, to imposed moralities, to the idea that there is no other way. Saying no is a powerful first step, but too much of no makes you sour and tired and reactionary; eventually your voice gets hoarse and after a while when nothing seems to change you forget why it even matters. You're so busy saying no, you haven't got time to say anything else. So Kika and I are learning to say yes to everything in our lives, to say it with our whole bodies, the contagious way of singing it out from our guts with our heads thrown back, swinging our hips up to the sky: yes! Yes! YES! I want to learn to sing a chorus of Yesses that follow the Nos: yes to building our own choices, our own visions and dreams and ideas, even though they may fail. Yes to our loves and our strange salvaged lives. Instead of saying "No that isn't enough," I want to say "Yes we can make it more."

This is what Charlotte and Uwe and the other twenty-some residents of the Kasa are saying: not just "No we won't leave," but "Yes we have the right to stay and make our lives this way." Kasa de la Muntanya itself is the consequence of saying yes to a dream of resistance and refusing to be moved from it.

"We will resist. We're not the kind to give up without the fight." Charlotte grinned, turning her face back toward the city spreading out across the hills, falling away into the ocean by the last light of day. "We can't give up the view here, can we?"

Fr nightmares & daydreams >>>

"This *cala* is the best on the coast," Nuri promised us. She was going home for the weekend, leaving the Keimada flat for the small coastal town where she'd grown up. She and Dani would drop us off at their secret spot on the ocean.

"There's a hut there, *una casa de los pescadoros*," Dani added, "You can stay there, no problem."

It sounded perfect, a quaint abandoned cottage on the sea, white sand and warm water. Barcelona was lodged in our lungs, tarry in our throats and thick on our pallid skin. City dust. Hibickina and I had taken more showers during our stay at the Keimada flat than either of us had in ages, but there are some things water can't wash off. At the *cala* we would lounge in the sparkling luxury of our daydreams, swim by moonlight and walk the shores in solitude. I couldn't wait.

An old woman and her middle-aged daughter, drinking wine and laughing together, were the only people there when we arrived. Hibickina and I left our packs in the *pescadoros'* hut and smiled at them as we followed Dani and Nuri further down the beach.

"Aqui, aqui es lo mejor," Nuri called over her shoulder, already peeling off layers of clothes. I shelled off my own filthy rags and poured my body into the water. It met me like an old lover, salty and familiar, the surprising remembrance of weightlessness. Here was Spain as I had imagined it from

childhood. Nutmeg and aquamarine, generous with the moon, easy with laughter, offering up the waters of myth.

Dani and Nuri left us in quiet, buoyed rapture. When our skin had finally raised chill bumps, Hibickina and I shivered our way back to the *pescadoros'* hut, where wine was waiting on the table, a ripe melon and two plump cloves of garlic. The women we'd seen earlier were gone, but I could almost hear their chuckles out along the tide.

We took the wine down to the sand, sat sipping and toasting, then lay there hanging wishes on shooting stars and plotting a message for the bottle. Sleep caught us in a sand cradle, held us close against her starry breast.

Sometime during the night they brought the body. We stayed frozen in still terror while they dragged it past us, leaving a long indentation in the sand. It was wrapped in dirty thick white canvas and whoever it was must've been heavy because it took about six shadowy figures to carry them. On the far side of the cove they scuttled about in the darkness. We stopped breathing as they began to dig. At a certain point we stopped watching, just buried ourselves beneath our gritty sleeping bags and prayed. How could we've been so stupid to fall asleep?

Fire cackled and spat madly. They were building a fire? We peeked out from beneath our bags. A pyre for the body probably. Burning it was smarter than burying it. Best to just stay still, not attract too much attention to ourselves. The old theory of "the monsters will go away if I don't move" was making a strong comeback. Why were they all laughing? Jesus Christ, sick fucks!! They were drinking beer and joking while their victim roasted, like it was a goddamn party.

Finally, out of exhaustion and lack of better options, we went back to sleep, only to be woken later by a smattering of rain which urged us into the hut for shelter. The killers were gone, but there were other adversaries to contend with. A militia of ants had discovered our melon and were colonizing the floor. Soon they were colonizing us.

Morning found us gritting our teeth. Not because of the nightmare we'd witnessed—because of the floor of the *pescadoros'* hut, the filth of which was undeniable by daylight. It was more than the ants. A patina of dirty sand, ashes, rancid oil, and meat grease lay congealed beneath our sleeping bags. The picnic table, sweet and welcoming in yesterday's twilight, was by day visibly encrusted with the thick and anonymous remains of many picnics. An indeterminate sludge oozed down its legs.

We set immediately to cleaning. I didn't even get all the way through dressing, just threw on my tank top and picked up a broom. The way I saw it, we could have the hut sparkling in half an hour and then enjoy paradise from inside as well as out. Affection for our little home grew in me as we scrubbed it clean with newspaper sponges, straightened the fireplace, hung our sleeping bags and clothes to air out. We swept every corner, organized our small kitchen of two blades and a torn sack of groceries, made plates of clean cardboard for ourselves.

I was out tidying the stoop when our first visitor arrived. It was the trash man, come to collect an overflowing barrel. That's normal, I thought. Dani and Nuri had assured us it would be quiet here, but over the weekend it probably saw more traffic. Today was Monday. Soon the trash man would finish and we could haunt the beach alone. As I swept, I tried not to feel self-conscious about my bare ass; after all, we'd been told it was a nudist spot, he was probably used to it. So I just gave him a cheerful wave while Hibickina sat inside, muffling delighted snorts at my predicament. The trash man took a long time doing his job, tediously arranging the load in the bag, sealing it with a progression of knots so intricate I wondered if he'd gone to the naval academy to learn them.

He must've worried that it was weird to stare without making conversation, so he asked me how long we'd been traveling.

"Ten years," I hissed back politely, baring my teeth at him in a war grin. "We travel from town to town giving karate lessons."

More knots as that sunk in, and finally he slung the sack over his uniformed shoulder and left, just as a fellow nudist came down the path, headed straight for me. The inopportune location of the hut became suddenly clear. It was impossible to get to the beach without passing directly by our open-air fourth wall. Human curiosity demanded that passersby look in on the hut, which they probably expected to be empty, or maybe being used for a family barbeque. Instead they saw us.

The fellow nudist smiled in comaraderie, enjoying the pleasures of exhibition. I avoided glancing at his pubic hair and reached for my shorts. I was not who he thought I was, just a woman who had woken up on a dirty floor and started sweeping before she remembered to get dressed.

Shoot. Nudists I did not mind, but lechers I did not like. Two in five minutes was not a good sign.

Another fifteen minutes and several families of tourists had arrived, each gaping in at us as they passed by. It seemed impossible that they would keep coming to such a remote location on an overcast Monday morning, but they continued to trickle in, and soon the beach was flooded. A formerly boarded-up snack bar that we'd assumed was defunct was now blaring tinny music and serving up cokes. The sand was a spread of sunglasses, towels, toys and invariably swimsuited bodies. We sat staring across the table at each other in disbelief. This was Paradise in the daytime?

Our hut seemed like the safest place to stay. I wasn't relishing the thought of swimming in my thick denim cutoffs with the bikinied masses out front any more than I had relished the thought of comparing pubic hair with the early-bird nudist who had long since mysteriously disappeared. Fuck it, we thought, opening our journals. Let's get some coffee and wait for evening.

Since we didn't feel up to participating in the neon spandex carnival that was happening outside, we decided to conjure up our own little faerie tale, taking our tag pens to the walls and inscribing them with scraps of poetry. Hibickina laid wood for the night's fire and I made a mobile of salvaged treasures, worn glass and bones strung on webs of dental floss. We dug out our skirts and sat like queens in scavenged splendor while we read each other stories.

Every two minutes another family passed over our stoop and gawked at the faeries in the fishbowl. Sometimes the parents smiled at us or pointed out a piece of the poetry to each other, other times they turned their faces quickly away. Their children invariably ventured closer. For a couple of hours this was extremely funny. After that I began to realize that our fishbowl was actually television and our faerie tale had become a bad sitcom. It was time to change the channel.

We left the cool beachfront and walked up the arid mountainous road. Costa Brava had gone months without rain, and the leaves of every tree on the *montaña* were layered with dust, aging the already sepia landscape. From the back seat of Nuri's car I'd spied the remains of an abandoned house, and now we made our way through curtains of dead blackberry tentacles toward its ruined doorway. Stiff and thorny, they left tracks of blood on our skin, which dried fast in the hot sun, branded us with our own iron.

The massive house was made of maize-colored stone, and its ancient walls were being swallowed by the soily mouth of Spain. Sly fingers of ivy had worked their way through the mortar and stolen its strength completely. The roof was only a memory of rotting beams, a few still crossing the sky in crooked lines above us, but most of them lying in skeletal piles on the dappled dirt floor. Fig leaves wound their way through the rusting metal window bars, ghosts of banquets past. We explored everywhere that the guardian blackberries would allow us, careful not to wake the sleeping spiders, reverent of the story traced by gilded rays in the dust beneath our tiptoeing feet.

This is why I love abandoned houses, I thought, why I have always loved them, from the very first one that I lived in as a child. It's because there is promise of home-to-come built into a story of home-that-was, a foundation that you are given but can change without weakening. It is a home that could be anybody's, anyone willing to accept the scarred walls and smeary or absent windows, anyone willing to live with creaking history and plant the present in its soil. It is saying, if you can see the garden I could become, I will be yours.

In silence we returned to the *pescadoros'* hut, each lost in our own thoughts, leftover fragments of light distilling the air.

Most of the tourists had gone, and the beach bar was closing up, so I went to ask if there was any coffee they might be throwing away. I sat drinking it on the stoop, watching the coral of the sky bloom gold and chestnut and peach, meet the rocky outcroppings of the shoreline. The light slid, the last of its palest yellow caught on the sailboats gliding by, turning their hulls to feathers and their canvas to wings. It was the hour when, from the right angle, the bellies of seagulls look the color of aged roses, but from any other angle they are already silhouettes.

It's not so much a faded light as a dusty one, I thought as Hibickina lit the fire, a self-satisfied light resting on the eves of a day well spent. Maybe I understand the idea of heaven. Not a place you go or make up in your mind, not a blinding whiteness but the path of the light as it traces your own hours in the place you are. Heaven, a place that you actually allow yourself to be, because you learn how to say YES! to life. You learn how to ask for free coffee when someplace is closing and you learn how to grin when they also hand you a cup of sugar and a sack of bread. We are playing house here, but more than that we are playing home. We have transformed space and lived in it. We would do this anywhere. Anywhere we go we will clean a little or a lot, make some food and make some magic, learn about love and revolution from whatever surrounds us. Anywhere we go, we will make gardens with whatever seeds are available to us.

The sea was maybe ten meters away, everyone but Hibickina and I was gone, and all I could hear were the sounds of fire and water. Inside, the capering flames warmed the dingy stones and the smoke chased away the mosquitoes, and outside the stars pricked holes in the black blanket of night. I was measuring the steady blink blink of the light-house when I remembered the body.

"Hib!"

She looked up from tending the fire, followed my pointing finger out to where we had witnessed the scene of the crime the night before. Horror lit her eyes. Together we crossed the curving expanse of sand, where the beached tourists had laid all day. At the far end of the curve, where we were sure the pyre had been, there was nothing but more sand. Gingerly we poked it with our toes. A few crusty coals lay nestled under the surface. No teeth, no femurs, not even a nail. Had we dreamed it? Had we both had the same ghoul-ish nightmare?

Suddenly, simultaneously, humiliatingly, the light dawned.

"Wood."

"Yeah. A lot of it."

"A lot of wood is heavy."

"And lumpy too."

"Ain't much wood around here."

"Pretty smart to haul it in."

"Shit! Shit! I can't believe we thought that . . ."

We lay cackling on the cooked bones of our imagina-tions, swearing we would never tell anyone how ridiculous we were, whooping at the stars, cursing and hollering.

In the morning, before the beach filled up, I walked down the shore and swam out to a small island of rocks. It was easy swimming, calm water warm enough to stave off shivering for quite a while. Salty but clean, cleaner than the dirty seawater of Barcelona which stung our eyes and chafed our skin with factory sludge, chemicals and other toxins.

Out on the island rocks I felt water-new, just-born the way I do when I am returned to my body, dripping and woken. I surveyed the dream that was my day, the shoreline towns in the distance, the perfect blue horizon, the boats and the green wall of pine trees beyond the beach. More nutmeg, more aquamarine, more myth and moon. Nothing to do but stretch in the breeze, with all of beauty and possibility spread out around me, all promises and no demands and fresh salt drying on my skin. It *was* a daydream. Somehow I had stolen through the gates of time while the guards slept; I had outsmarted banks and logic and all the pessimistic realists in the world and swum like a mermaid to the edges of my own daydream. But even while I felt the warmth of fantasy shine with the sun on my skin, I also realized that the daydreams I have are only differentiated from reality by space and distance. On second glance the rocks around me were covered in seagull shit, people on the boats passing by were staring at me, and in one of the rocky pockets where water was caught there was a strange pool of dark pink liquid which betrayed the purity of nature. Look again, and the very body which had happily swum me out to the rocks was the same one that sometimes pained me for the ways it deviated from magazine pages; a body that looked nothing like a mermaid, yet there it was, naked and wet on the shit-encrusted rocks at the edges of a Mediterranean daydream.

Daydreams are really only life, when you live them up close, I thought. Take away the distance, live daily in the beauty you had imagined from afar, and immediately the flaws surface. It's like love that way; once you arrive, once you are firmly aground in a love, you begin to see that it has cracks and rough edges and dirty spots, pockets of toxins, less privacy, maybe, than what you had imagined. But if you are willing to remember the initial distant beauty of a love or a daydream, and if you are willing to live in that beauty up close even with all its imperfections . . . then the dream is yours to have. People who can remember that on a daily basis are lucky, because they get to spend their time swimming and kissing instead of always looking off into the distance, making up things that aren't necessarily true about places or people who are far away. It's almost too easy to avoid living the dream you are in while questing for one more perfectly imagined. Half of being a dreamer is dreaming and half of it is actually living in your dreams.

huck finn revisited

The ocean was a few days behind us, and freeway rhythm was back, or at least it would've been if someone would stop for us. Our morning ride had left us at the most impossible hitchhiking location, where cars were going by so fast that I was actually afraid for my life. Even an optimist would conclude that there was pretty much nowhere for them to safely pull over, and I was already wilting in the heat and exhaust. The only thing in my stomach was defeat, since the ants had stolen most of our grapes while we'd slept the night before, or at least closed our eyes against the horrid neon hiss of the gas station lights which glared at us through a thin screen of trees. Now we were huddled up against a guardrail with eighteen inches of shoulder between us and the freeway, and it seemed like probably we would die right there, one way or another.

"I wish, I wish, I wish I wish, oh I wish somebody would fucking rescue us . . ." came our discordant lament, fully aware that we might have to walk a Very Long Time to get out of this situation.

Just then a small car swerved impulsively to the thin

shoulder, and out climbed a beautiful man with laughing-crow eyes and golden skin. He opened the hatchback, cast a wary glance at the freeway, and started rearranging his brimming auto to make room for us. His little BMX bike was piled on top of boxes of fruit and veggies from his parents' garden, which were stacked on crates of tools and other miscellaneous items. He handed me a snorkel, then a tomato, a wrench . . . diligently he worked, carving out room for us and our packs. He'd forgotten his car was full when he'd stopped, he said, but now that he was here, he wouldn't leave without us.

Somehow we got it all arranged, piled in and started driving. Michel was coming from the coast, where he'd been diving. He always stopped in to visit his parents on his return trip, he smiled, nodding his head at the wobbling tower of produce in the back. He excavated a big bottle of organic juice from under the seat and offered us sips.

"My mother is into organics."

I let the sweet rich nectar slide down my throat and said with happy certainty, "I think I'd like your mother."

Then I realized that what I'd said sounded vaguely like a marriage proposal and I blushed, and he laughed and told us more about his whole foods mania, and his father, who was Catalan. They'd often driven Michel down these same winding rural highways when he was a child, passed through the same endless acres of sunflowers that stood in banks of yellow, their laughing heads thrown back against the sky. It made him nostalgic, and he took thick drinks of the clean mountain air, reminisced about walking through the hillsides of Foix when he was young. He was half with us and half suspended in the silky threads of his sunlit past, occasionally sending postcards of memory across the gearshift and over to the passenger seat.

We neared our turnoff. He knew of a good place to put us, he said—so far nobody ever dropped us off in Europe, they simply "put us" places—one just around the corner, where we'd be certain to get a ride. But as he was describing it he looked around and noticed the road was empty.

"I tell you this," he said, "when there is not one car."

"Don't worry," I assured him, "it will change."

He cocked his head, why so certain? And I explained, "I think if you think about something long enough, you can sometimes make it happen."

"Ahhh," he said, "you thought about me and I stopped."

We both laughed at his joke but I felt so at home among the tools and crates of apples, sailing through the sea of sunflowers, that I thought, maybe so. Maybe that's how destiny works, matching up memory postcards with people whose address is General Delivery.

"So why are you traveling like this?" Michel asked, as we disentangled our packs from his bicycle wheels at a ghosted gas station. He knew they were all we had, smaller than those of most travelers, and as we strapped them onto our dirty hips our scrappy pads belied the nature of our sleeping quarters. He handed us each an apple from the crate.

"Have you ever read *Huck Finn*?" I asked him.

Michel nodded, smiling.

"Well, when we were young, we read all those books, looking for girls in their pages," I told him. "But we couldn't find anything. We don't want to be the boring girls that the boys in adventure stories get crushes on. We wanted to have our own adventure stories.

"So we're gonna make some new pages," I finished, biting through the taut ruby skin and into its sweet blank flesh.

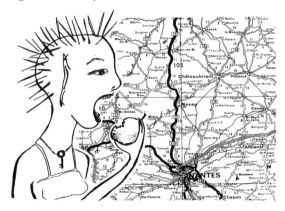

lunch with the dead

Up in the hills above Foix, there's a classic castle keeping its wary eye on the town. Though in fact there isn't much to be wary of, just a few quiet winding streets, one small and well-behaved river, strings of tidy old buildings well-settled on their foundations, not likely to go anywhere.

There's also a cemetery in Foix, I shouldn't forget that, though as Americans mostly we don't like to talk about our dead. When somebody we love dies, we shell out money for a service devoid of real emotion, presided over by some crank who never met the deceased. Then we stuff what's left of them in a box or a bag and leave them to rot—or not, given the nasty lasting effects of chemical preservatives—and rarely go to the same spot again. Maybe once a year on Memorial Day when we drop off a wreath of plastic flowers, a pale imitation of what used to be loving libations.

But this was France, where death has a more esteemed position. Parisian cemeteries are famous for being parks as well as bone yards, and the final resting places of the dead, at least the famous ones, are memorialized by tourists. Or vandalized by locals, as the case may be, but either way not forgotten entirely. In that spirit, we thought, why not take advantage of a quiet spot to pass the sunny afternoon?

We strolled between the graves until we found a comfortable, slightly unkempt plot, surrounded by a rusting iron fence vined with purple morning glories. A narrow gate hung slightly open on crooked hinges; obviously it was meant for the absent grave-tender, but we laughed to think the resident might be coming and going as well. We set up camp underneath a willow tree at the foot of the tomb and began spreading out a picnic of our staple foods: ripe avocados and carrots, garlic, fresh crusty bread, then shiny sharp pocket knives to cut it all and rich dark chocolate for dessert.

As we ate, we looked around at the tidy graveside shrines, fresh bright flowers and the burned-down stubs of votive candles. Nary a plastic wreath in sight. I noticed happily that almost all of the tombs were being cared for; it was reassuring to see that the dead aren't always immediately forgotten. I'd like to think it's the same with the living, that I'm not forgotten as soon as I disappear from the horizon of my friends' daily lives. Sometimes it's easier to hold on to distant people that way . . . easier, but you don't always leave them room to change without you.

"Kika," I said abruptly. "I'm glad our friends aren't dead."

She looked at me in horror. That hadn't come out quite how I intended.

"I just mean . . . Well in a certain way it's almost like they're dead, for now, because we haven't talked to them in so long. Sometimes I imagine that they are dead, you know, and it's like they're with us, like ghosts, or guardian angels even."

Kika arched an eyebrow at me. Oh dear. What was I saying?

"I'm glad you're not dead, too," I concluded lamely. She looked at me calmly. "Well, Hibickina, I'm glad you're not dead, too."

We burst into mad laughter. Sometimes it seemed like all the translating—English to Spanish, Spanish to French, our private language into anything commonly understandable—it was only making my communication skills worse.

We were still sprawled in the grass, clutching our sides, when the groundskeeper and self-appointed security guard approached us, smiling warily. He furrowed his brow as he began with real concern, "Madamoiselle . . ." I tried to stop laughing long enough to at least give the appearance of taking him seriously. He seemed to be saying that we couldn't stay here, as the old people were quite disturbed by our picnicking here. What old people? I looked around the cemetery for irate geriatric French couples, but we were the only ones there apart from the groundskeeper.

"They're very old," our new friend was saying, "and they have their traditions." Who did he think we were bothering? The corpses were probably happy to have some company.

"Of course they're old!" I blurted in English. "They're all dead!"

The groundskeeper had grown very perturbed, and was now implying that whoever it was we'd disturbed might call the police. I wondered if the local *gendarmerie* had a direct line to the underworld.

"We'll go, thanks so much for your trouble," I reassured him, "we'll go right away." I reached for my shoes. Placated, his smile reappeared and he wandered off between the tombstones and angels. I put my shoes down and settled back into the shady spot against the fence. I watched Kika trying to stifle her peals of laughter, her bright skin made brighter in the sunlight. This is how we should all look, settled among the dead, like grounded angels.

13 august

Buildings are the places we construct
our lives around, central to the
way we see the world. How does it
shape us to walk past ancient castles
in the countryside, old plazas & older
houses in the city? What does it do
to our sense of history, of continuity?
And when they're juxtaposed with glass
and steel, the hurried halfway
constructions made more from money
than any kind of art, drawn from
computer plans and built with diesel-
fueled machines... Easy to forget that
human hands ever had any part in it.

Graffiti scrawled on the oldest walls -
is it a refusal to let history have its
way with us?

In America we see almost nothing that
outlives us, "old" does not seem to
exist. We see the passing years as
terrorists, and it becomes easy to destroy
our aging selves the way we destroy
our aging buildings. The young can't
learn from the old, can't move in and
inhabit their stories unless it's done
secretly, in darkness, under lock & key.
Who loves old buildings in America?
  Anything ramshackle is razed before
we have time to make it into something
new. Even here in Europe there seems
to be less & less room for reclamation:
new E.U. laws push everyone out from
the old; inhabited or not, faded buildings
are demolished to make room for new
investments, the same way local cultures
are drowning in a homogenized market.

26 august

pieces of old rubber, bent nails, disintegrating magazines with their rotting covers leaving only traces of the model's face, soggy cardboard and scraps of cloth and lone shoes. The flattened form of a rabbit, the cotton of its tail still wagging in the engine-made wind. A crushed hawk, its feathers splayed out among its guts in a broken promise of sky, silky sand colored wings fluttering from hunks of raw flesh.

you can learn so much just from walking alongside the highway. It's the dust under our collective bed, the underside of society's couch cushions. It's the fray at the edges of our order and whether we like it or not, it tells our secrets.

there are all sorts of rusty pieces of metal there, not just pop cans and random bits of steel but bolts and nuts and washers, hints that things aren't always held together as well as they seem to be, and that when you hurtle along at 75 mph you have no way of knowing when or why they start to fall apart. moving so fast, most people can't even see what's broken.

* start small *

once there was a girl who saw the moon. From far off it looked like something she could touch or taste and she spent years

staring up at the sky, trying to figure out how to arrange her strength so that she could get what she wanted.

she tried from many angles... sometimes she got sleepy waiting.

the moon kept on moving through its seasons as she watched in stillness.

nothing seemed to move inside her. what was wrong?

she made wishes on fast-moving shooting stars, whispering teach my feet to move like that...

WAtching

waiting

years she spent on the edges of things, watching them move: people, cities, the weather.

thinking, if only i could make use of my strength...

until:

one day, she looked down and noticed a small weed growing up through the cracks around her island of pavement. Even though it was daylight, it gave her that same curious feeling as the moon, and on instinct she bent to reach it.

she took it between her fingers and the small seeds caught in the wind like shooting stars. It was the lightest, most possible dream she could imagine, wild and growing and small. but when she looked down at her feet, it grew bigger in her hands.

i do make love

The punk community in Rennes obviously had some roots. It had been around long enough for gardens to get planted, babies to get born, graffiti galleries to stake strongholds. There was a big *te t' aime*—love yourself—scrawled on a wall and as we stood gazing at it, it seemed possible to both Hibickina and I that we had discovered a place where a scene had turned into a movement. The scene was still the medium, but the politics of love and anarchy were clearly in motion, opening up secret doorways, and Rennes was swinging on their hinges.

There were punks everywhere—older punks with babies sitting at sidewalk cafes, intellectual punks reading liberation literature in the parks, punks on bikes. Grungy street punks with skin disease sat idly on curbsides with their herds of dogs, scratching themselves. When the police came by and told them they had to go, they'd say "*oui, oui,* we'll move," and remain there, comfortably, as the cops went around the corner: this was ritual.

It was nice to have a rest from the constant stares we were used to. Hibickina and I were crustier than old bread. We had plunged the depths of grime: the word had to be remodeled to make room for us. But in Rennes, no one looked twice at the grey cylinder posing as my neck or held back their smiles because of the faded raggedy tank tops welded over our pungent dirt-streaked skin.

As we were hitching out of town, some guy in a shiny car slowed to ask where we were going, and hissed in a thick French accent, "Do you make love?"

We were shocked into delayed reaction, and then chased him down the street with raised middle fingers slammed against our forearms: Extra Fuck You.

"Jesus Christ," said Hibickina after our initial anger had turned into amusement. "I can't believe that happens even when we look like this."

"Yeah, and that asshole actually seemed to expect an answer."

"That's what's funny . . . Do these men actually think we're going to respond? Like do they really think we're gonna turn around and come running to them like dogs when they call out at us and say oh yes, I'd love to suck your cock?"

"I don't know." Now I was laughing really hard.

We stood there taking turns calling to each other, imitating our own imaginations, panting, yes please, yes please, please let me do you . . .

Soon we were doubled over with hysterics, drooling, *here pussy pussy*, falling over on our packs in loud whooping howls, *c'mon pussy, yes sir, I do make love sir . . .*

These are the chapters that *Huck Finn* never had.

i say mermaid

The windows were open so I had a kind of windblown quiet in the back seat, perfect for watching the sun set. When it had slid all the way off the horizon the leftover light spun watercolors across the sky. At first it was just shades of salmon, some cherry and periwinkle colors streaking out into vague water lines, but then the mermaid started taking shape. She was winged and arched and swimming, and it looked like she had freed a flock of birds, like they had flown in ripples from her fingers. She kept transforming; more wings, less water, more water, less wings. Less human and then more. Always strong, gliding and reaching.

I watched her for a long while from the lulling jounce of the back seat. She spooned light over me like honey, the nectar of truth after all those billboard images forced into my eyes. Cities and towns, gas stations and freeways, the billboards of corporate mythology are inescapable. Their vast monopoly on images becomes the ruling faerie tale of modern times. The mythical story of money, perfection, and power assigns to us our desires, values, and destinies. But the mermaid filled a space the billboards could never claim, the wide open sky from which she was spun and the close of the light into which she swam. Even after she disappeared from my dusty window her form stayed, pressed strong against my eyes. When I closed them I could still see her, translucent fingers, periwinkle sternum, flying through streams of cherries and roses.

The loss of magic has a lot to do with the loss of imaging. When those billboards are all we see, of course they become our faerie tales. We stop noticing anything else and believe them. If we want a different story, we have to replace the images of money and perfection with new ones. We have to show ourselves pictures of new things to believe in. Sometimes making new images means using our hands creatively and living our life loudly outside the lines. And sometimes it just means learning how to really see the world from your own angle: some would say sunset, but I say mermaid. The new images we make or see create room for characters nobody has written before, faces nobody has captured, destinies free of certainty. When we remake our images we remake our selves. We leave a little less room for perfection and a little more room for magic.

 le wagon.

We never did figure out how to pronounce "St. Brieuc." For hundreds of kilometers, in every car we had the same exchange:

"We're going to St. Brieuc."

"Where?"

"St. Brieuc!"

"Where?" Finally light dawned over drivers' perplexed expressions, and they'd say, "Oh, you mean St. BRIEUC!" pronouncing the word exactly the same way we'd just said it, like a bubble of tar sliding down the back of your throat. Then they'd laugh and shake their heads, saying, "No, no, your accent is cute. Really."

Then, very often, the puzzled look returned to their faces as they asked, "Why on Earth are you going *there?*" As we thumped along in the back of his van, one guy told us with a shuddering sort of smile. "I was born in St. Brieuc . . . but I got the hell out." Perhaps this should have served as some sort of clue, but we just smiled back at him blithely.

Sometimes we just told them we were going to Mt. St. Michel and had some time to kill before we met our friend outside Paris. Sometimes we explained about the train squat, Le Wagon, that had inspired us all the way back in Belgium.

We were following only the roughest of directions to Le Wagon, but we were certain, from Kimmi's description, it couldn't be too hard to find. It didn't seem to matter to either of us that it was late at night and growing later, that St. Brieuc appeared to be a small industrial wasteland reeking of fish guts and diesel fuel, or that we were traveling on a map made solely from instinct and goodwill. We were singing as we headed down the hill toward Port Legué, skipping unevenly under the weight of our packs.

It was quiet when we got to the water. Darkened houseboats and small trawlers were moored along one edge of the wide canal, tired old canoes and broken boat carcasses beached on the steep cement slope of the far side. The boats rubbed shoulders soundlessly like tethered horses.

"Oh, look at this old yacht!" Kika cried, pointing to a delapidated old tugboat painted in loud red and yellow. Without a second thought, she slipped over its side and settled happily on the splintered deck.

"Are you hungry?" she asked brightly, already pulling bread and apples and rich golden couscous from the depths of her pack. "Let's make a picnic!"

We ate leaning against the ribs of the boat, rocking gently and watching the stars sag sleepily overhead. Occasionally cars would careen wildly around the corner and zoom off up the hill, creatures from a completely different world, but for the most part the balmy night was ours alone. It was hard to believe that we ever had another life before this one.

We considered sleeping there in Kika's yacht, but we were finally drawn on again by the thought of the train squat; gardens, friendly dogs, hot coffee if we were lucky. We asked the first passing stranger if we were headed in the right direction—everyone in St. Brieuc knows about Le Wagon, we'd been assured. (This did turn out to be true, but not for the reasons we'd expected.) The guy cocked his eyebrow at us.

"You wanna buy hash?"

What? No, we want to stay there!

"Oh. Well it's this way, yeah. Far, though." He stalked off, leaving us with our first inkling of suspicion.

We walked. We walked and walked, with the black and gold canal on one side and the train tracks on the other, silos and factory stacks and abandoned buildings poking up all around us. Finally, we came across an inhabited building that did seem to be a squat covered in graffiti and sloppy circled A's, it looked like a former factory, a dirty brick structure with lots of boarded windows, moored in an ocean of broken glass and concrete.

"That can't possibly be Le Wagon. It must be a different squat," Kika said a little flatly. Where were the boxcars? There wasn't a garden, there wasn't even a yard, just asphalt and trash and the flickering blue light from a T.V.

We eyed it silently for a few minutes before she said, more firmly, "That *can't* be Le Wagon. Besides, didn't that guy just say it was really far?"

We kept walking.

When you are already running on Neptunian time, it's easy not to notice that it's getting very late in terms of the regular clock, and when you're very tired it's easy not to notice you're not thinking clearly. When you're already busy living outside the boundaries of convention, it's easy not to notice that you're doing things that might be considered . . . well, stupid. That's how we ended up in the mouth of a very long, very dark train tunnel in the middle of the night, discussing whether or not we should walk through to the other side. The road had split at least half a mile back, and, having no idea which way to go, we compromised by following the railroad tracks out into the deserted woods. Our logic was that, since the road hadn't led us to the train squat, we might be able to get there by following the tracks.

However, the tracks only took us deeper into the lonely trees, and finally brought us to the gaping black maw of the tunnel. Our puny flashlight beams were swallowed in its darkness. We stood debating; on one hand, it might not be the wisest course of action to follow the train tracks—which were clear of debris and obviously still in use—into a narrow tunnel of unknown length and uncertain destination. On the other hand, though, what if the house was just on the other side of a short passage, and we let ourselves be deterred by a few meters of darkness? Would we allow our quest for this amazing squat to be derailed by the mere prospect of messy death under the wheels of a speeding train?

In the end, we were deterred only because our consultation was interrupted by a loud noise from the bushes. There was an abrupt rustle of leaves, followed by a breaking of sticks and a distinctly human whisper.

"What did you just say?" I hissed. Kika shook her head. "It wasn't me."

Clearly, we were not alone.

We looked down the tunnel. Indecipherable pitch black. We looked back up the track, the way we'd come. Beyond the edge of the woods we could still see the reassuring yellow glow of the streetlights.

"Maybe we should go back and check the upper road."

"Yeah, let's do that." We were trying to act casual. We were scared shitless. Kika hefted her pack and strode away with the gait of a boy.

We followed the high road all the way to its exhausting conclusion in the upper-class suburbs of the next town, where we were confronted by an endless string of modern stucco monstrosities, walled in behind individual security fences. Oh, good, just what we were looking for. I was beginning to wonder if Le Wagon was anything more than a collective hallucination.

We were desperately thirsty and out of water. Our last detour had taken us straight up the side of a small mountain, and we licked our lips sadly with dry tongues as we eyed the water bottles emptied hours ago. This was definitely not the sort of neighborhood whose residents take kindly to black-clad, pack-toting crusty kids traipsing through their yards at all hours of the night, but neither had they seen fit to provide any conveniently located water fountains. Consequently, we felt entitled to make use of a garden hose in one of the well-manicured lawns. Kika slipped easily over the fence into the nearest yard and nosed around—but there was no hose, no spigot. Same at the next house, and the next, and the next after it. What was going on here anyway? These were stately doctor's homes, with wide green lawns, tidy flower beds, window boxes full of lush geraniums. Where the hell were all the water hoses? This wasn't America, it wasn't possible that everyone paid a lawn service to come water for them. It was at this point in my whispered tirade, stomping through some rich family's rose garden, that I stumbled into a rain barrel and received a crash course in the graywater systems of northwest France.

It seemed highly unlikely that Le Wagon would be nestled in among these suburban gardens. We were beyond tired at this point, devoid of patience, and completely disinterested in the prospect of sleeping out in one of the fenced-in, hoseless yards, so we decided to head back to the fork and try our luck along the lower road. Yet, much like the train tracks, this road also seemed destined to take us the long way to nowhere. To keep up our sagging spirits as we walked, Kika decided this would be the ideal time to tell me all the horrible crime stories she knew about the woods around the town where she grew up. Small towns are dangerous places. People get bored and they get drunk. Her town was a lot like this one, she said.

"This doesn't scare you, does it?" she asked hopefully.

"Oh no, not at all, really," I assured her as I checked over my shoulder for the sixteenth time.

Suddenly, I froze. There was a familiar roar coming up behind us. On the way up the hill to our garden tour, we'd been passed three or four times by what appeared to be the same car, speeding by at about 150 km/hr and each time forcing us up onto the shoulder of the road. There was no shoulder here, there was a sheer cliff on one side and a deep patch of stinging nettles and briar bushes on the other. I looked back and saw the headlights growing bigger at an incalculable rate. We were living in a nightmare. "Jump!" Kika shouted, pulling me into the thorns just as the diabolical car sped by centimeters from our toes.

Lying on our backs in the nettle patch, both of us felt inclined to give up entirely. *Where was the fucking train squat?* Defeated, we were finally forced to concede that the sorrowful-looking building we'd passed hours ago was, most likely, the squat we'd come halfway across France to visit. I was beginning to feel a little sheepish about that fact.

"Maybe it's not what it looks like, maybe you just can't see their garden from the road," said Kika. Ever the optimist. In any case, it was probably the only place in a five mile radius where we could get potable water. We headed back down the steep hill, still pulling briars from our skin.

We got back to Le Wagon in the wee hours of the morning, but we could still see the flickering light of the T.V. through the windows. As we walked toward the house we were assailed by the powerful stink of large quantities of dog shit. Around back we found the train cars—not old boxcars like we'd imagined, but small compartment cars, like on the Paris metro. Still no gardens, though.

We knocked at a window, as there seemed to be no door, and a young punk stuck his head out, didn't say anything but raised his eyebrows at us. I was too tired and my French was too bad for politesse, so I just said, "My friend Kimmi told us about your squat. Can we sleep here tonight?" He shrugged and came around to the fence where two huge dogs waited, snarling. He sort of kicked them aside as he opened the gate for us, then shouted something that sent them whimpering away. We introduced ourselves and he grunted in response as he led us into the house. Inside, two other guys slumped on the couch. They didn't look away from the television.

Even within the punk scene, squats are not generally known to be bastions of cleanliness. You get used to this. But Le Wagon was, by far, the filthiest squat either of us had seen. Ever. Of course there were beer bottles and overflowing ash-trays, cigarette butts on the floor. The coffee table was hidden by several layers of dirty dishes, empty soda cans, spilled beer, dead fleas, and dog fur. A sickly yellow light hung buzzing from the center of the ceiling, silhouetting the pile of dead bugs that had collected in its bottom. The walls were covered in posters for hardcore shows, pictures of kids with mohawks and fifteen eyebrow rings, and a range of graffiti including the scrawled message, Drunk Punx Rock! There were a few requisite political flyers, as well. A thick membrane of ash and grime seemed to have settled over everyone and every-thing in the room. More than the dirt, though, it was really misery that coated the whole place. It seemed to catch in your throat like thick dust and leave you gasping for air as soon as you walked in the door. It isn't polite to ask strangers why they're so desperately unhappy, though, so we just filled our water bottles in the sticky kitchen—better not to turn on the light—and sat down.

Television, the great deadener. There was a movie just starting, an Italian remake of *The Phantom of the Opera* over-dubbed in French. It was basically a blend of gore and cheap tit shots, and the dialogue was so elementary even I could understand it.

The guy who'd let us in stood up and asked, "You wanna Coke? It's four francs." Kika and I shook our heads in unison. He shoved the dogs out of his way as he left with a shrug.

Okay, so this was not the place we'd expected. So be it. Still, I didn't want to be unkind, I wanted to be interested and appreciative. After all, we'd searched this place out because we were fascinated by the lives people made for themselves in the cracks of business-as-usual, we thought we could gather some kind of tools or inspirations from Le Wagon. Besides, whatever the state of the place, they didn't have to let us sleep here. But the truth of it was, these boys were busy being typically numbed by a typical sexist movie, and I'd be lucky if I got out of this house without contracting scabies. All I wanted was to go to sleep and dream about happy squats in happy boxcars with happy dogs.

When he came back, Dog Kicker led us to our quarters in one of the small compartment cars. It smelled like a blend of diesel fuel, dirty dog, and rank human sweat, and we carefully spread out our foam pads on the bed before unrolling our sleeping bags. Please, please, please, I prayed to the far-away clean-looking moon as I drifted off to an oily sleep, don't let us get scabies.

In the morning, I stood up almost before my eyes were open. "Kika. Kika! It's morning." She groaned. "That means we can leave!" I said jubilantly. By the light of day, we could see more about our surroundings than either of us really wanted to know. We packed up our stuff in record time. We stepped out into the yard, looking around halfheartedly for Dog Kicker so we could say goodbye.

Suddenly, Kika stopped in front of me, so abruptly I

nearly ran into the back of her. Then she turned to me with a strange, dazed look in her eyes and a wheatpasted smile "Oh. My. God. Did you see the . . . that?" She was talking without moving her lips.

On the wall of the house was an enormous mural that showed a mohawked and pierced punk guy skanking wildly with a snaggly-toothed dog at his feet. I wondered if he was about to kick it. Off to one side, a boy pirate-punk with an eyepatch leapt out from a clump of bright green pot plants brandishing a stubbly sword. In between them hovered a punk fairy with poofy hair, long-lashed almond eyes, outrageous hips and breasts and a tiny waist. Her scanty purple dress was ripped across the front, revealing a perfectly round breast with a nipple ring, and her lips were pursed in a come-hither *O*. I looked back at Kika, who was still smiling like a corpse.

"I think I need to leave," she said. "Immediately. Before I become disrespectful."

Out on the road again, we stared at each other blankly. This was everything we were trying to figure out how to transform, it just happened to be wearing a more familiar costume.

"Oh, Hibickina . . ." Kika's party-hostess grin wasn't cracking and she still had that glazed look in her eyes. I wondered idly if the water at Le Wagon had been potable, after all.

"Well, Kika. *I'm* certainly glad our noble quest was successful. That wasn't just some filthy squat, you know, in spite of appearances to the contrary. That was a dream of Love and Freedom, damnit, it was a fortress of radical subjectivity, it was . . . it was . . ."

"An apathetic boys' clubhouse with soft porn on the walls?" The rictus grin had finally been replaced by her usual imp smile.

"Oh, but look!" She nodded at the patch of ground between us, where a few scraggly dandelions poked out between cracked asphalt and shattered beer bottles.

"We found the garden."

⟞ dol de bretagne ⟝

We were in yet another small town where evening was in full bloom, and rain had broken out. Northern France was closing its skies early. There was no salmony sunset that night, just cold wet bricks on either side of the covered archway we huddled under, and yellow-lit window squares softening the courtyard. The damp and grey almost made it feel like Olympia, but a sad faraway Olympia, where we had no friends, no one to offer hot soup or extra sweaters or say *hey do you wanna go see that movie at the Capitol Theater tonight?* The sound of the gutter waterfalls and mourning church bells might be romantic, I thought, but I suspect there may be better poetry to be made from the inside looking out, instead of shivering out here and wondering where the hell we're gonna sleep tonight.

But we did sit there shivering, huddled on our packs, writing by street lamp as the last of the light faded. A fat and bitchy black and white alley cat, come to sit in solidarity with us, yowled her misery at the rain. She had owl eyes and white whiskers, which stood out like moonbeams against the black night of her jaw, and she was apparently a regular at the little restaurant nearby. Its kitchen window opened out into the alley, across from our archway. Eyeing her paunch, we decided she had the right idea. A cup of leftover soup might heat up our insides enough to last through the night, we reckoned. We'd sit there until closing and then swallow down whatever they might give us before heading back out to search for shelter. Maybe the rain would've ebbed by then.

The lively clatter of the kitchen filled up the desolate courtyard, and the dish boy's song splashed out of his suds to the stream at our feet. I had filled my glass jar with hot water from a café earlier, and Hibickina and I passed the still-warm tea back and forth with rapt appreciation. Is this poetry? we asked ourselves. Black Georgian tea in a dark covered alley. A spot of warm in a vast wet cold. A singer and song. Was it?

The flow in the gutters became torrential. The church bells were lost in the current, but a roof in the rain was still an answered prayer. We sipped and sat, discussing gratitude, how much you learn to appreciate the little things when they are all you have. Our life, a series of grateful stanzas: *Oh thank you we have bread, Hibickina do you feel its chewy guts wrapped up in the fragrant crust? Mmmm and blackberries, found free alongside the highway . . . Ripe apples in accessible trees, look, this one has barely any scabs! Praise for clusters of grapes hanging over suburban fences, unexpected unexpected . . . Kika this must be the best coffee I've had in my entire life, eh? Hark, the joy of hidden meadows behind gas stations. The hymn of our sleeping pads, that quarter inch of packed foam which cradles us up from dog shit and dew . . . Did I mention my knife? It's sharp, Hib, let me cut that garlic, liberate its magic medicine, saving grace of the road wanderers, salvation in papery purple skin . . . Aren't we lucky to have healthy bodies and fed hearts? Aren't we aren't we aren't we? Ask and ye shall receive and if it is music and sunlight ye desire I will send down a convertible from heaven which will grace your thumbed prayer and for ten minutes will speed ye through a golden morning pumping irresistible dance music through a quintessentially divine sound system . . . Hallelujah, for I have found a place to pee and fill my water bottle . . .*

"So many people in this circuit get so stuck, so blackened and hollow . . ." Hib had sighed earlier. And when does the glory of gratitude wear off? Is it when the motion stops? When you are at home and still you have nowhere to go? It's never your city when you are locked out of it by the system of the city itself. It's easy to become contemptuous of a place which has no room for you, which bars you from your most basic needs. There have always been two cities, the visible and the invisible . . .

"Three," Hibickina reminds me firmly, "the one you see and the one you don't, and then the one you dream."

She sat next to me with two red curls escaping from her hood, casting shadows on her cheeks. The whole kitchen joined the dish boy's song and started to close. We could almost taste the soup . . .

We thought for sure the song would mean a kind yes, but no, no to the ratty strangers sitting out in the rain with the cat. No, no, no. So many locks. So many forbidden doorways. What is the spell of longing cast by those windows when it gets cold and they gleam with foggy light?

Earlier, Hibickina had spoken about the difference between poverty and feeling impoverished. It always comes down to having choices, we'd agreed, and we still have so many. What does it feel like, I asked her that night in the cold dark drear of Dol de Bretagne, to be a dreamer stuck on the streets with no allies and no way out?

But I knew, even without hearing the sentence. Like death, I answered myself. Like broken bottles which could've held dreams, like hawks flattened on the sides of freeways.

We traipsed in circles around the town, looking for elusive shelter. It felt like we walked half the night. No doorway to borrow 'till daylight, and it made me wonder if city planning committees intend it that way, if they design architectural safeguards against homeless populations. Finally we found a covered doorway on the outskirts, where across the parking lot a circus slept soundly in a spread of caravans, and we dreamt in more stanzas of gratitude: angels writing the poetry of *luchadoras*, eternal thanks resisting their own demise.

We woke to the circus packing up, feeding their lions in wrinkled pajamas, bringing in armloads of wet laundry hung too soon the night before, hung in blind faith. We watched them stumble through their coffee and cigarettes under bright plastic awnings droopy with rain, and the fiery magic makers looked just like anyone else.

Leaving, we walked through the wet morning grass to the chime of the church bells, and happened upon a campground. The restroom was unlocked, with free hot showers, peach painted walls, gleaming white tiles and pieces of the morning sky falling in clean rays through the skylights. We stood naked in our own private stalls, lost in water and light, we scoured ourselves and afterwards kept touching our new skin in awe.

climbing

I didn't know why I wanted to go to Mt. St. Michel. All I knew of it was what I'd seen in an American film, still images of a fortified medieval village, a tidal island breaking out of the grey coast of Bretagne. I thought it looked like somebody's idea of magic.

But as we traveled out the causeway we began to see another angle. In the parking lot, rows of shiny cars flashed brighter than the gold statue of St. Michel that crowned the abbey, and a sign advertising exchange rates greeted us as we approached the high town walls. The main gate opened into a wide cobbled courtyard occupied by a throbbing mass of tourists, including a group of fifty-some hyperactive school kids. Their shrieks and shouted insults echoed clearly off the stone walls; strangely incongruous to hear "Bite it, you stupid cow!" ringing through the narrow streets of a nine-hundred-year-old monastic village.

The eponymous mountain of St. Michel is in fact an enormous pyramidal rock, upon which the abbey was constructed at the pinnacle, closest to heaven, and the village later sprang up around the base. Unfortunately, the town now seemed to be very nearly at the gates of hell itself. Its streets were jammed with expensive cafés and boutiques full of historical souvenirs, all the houses seemed to have been converted into hotels or museums with high admission prices, and absolutely everything was for sale. I wondered how an entire small town had been converted into Ye Olde Medieval Shoppinge Malle. But once we climbed just a few flights of stairs up the terraced hillside, we left almost everyone behind.

We found a small tidy cemetery where I imagined the dead buried generations deep. Once, climbing up toward the sacred ground of the abbey must have felt like leaving behind the messy mire of human bodies for the pure terrain of the spirit; a mirror for the passage from life into eternal life-in-death, as the church would have it. This cemetery was just a stopping point along the way. Every grave was marked by at least one statue of Christ on the cross, cast in iron and accurate down to the last gruesome detail: the bleeding gash in his side, the agonized face with eyes imploring the sky, the skeletal outline of ribs and hips. Its precision made me think of relics kept from the smallest bits of saints: St. Joan's finger bone, a scrap from St. Vaclav's cloak. Why this obsession with the physical minutiae of gods and saints? The proof is in the details, they say; it's reassurance that the story is in fact history, that there's a reason to pack in with the Church. Otherwise, why bother with the climb?

When we finally came to the abbey itself, I was surprised to see that we'd have to pay for admission. A sign informed us, Your ticket price goes toward the upkeep of the abbey, each year it costs so many thousands of dollars, blah blah blah . . . and by the way, please be respectful as this is a building dedicated to the glory of God. I suppose there's a place for pragmatism even in the Lord's house, but wasn't it Christ who kicked the moneychangers out of the temple? Still, we shelled out our change and were herded along with a guided tour.

The guide was a wiry, animated Parisian man in his mid-fifties who proceeded to tell us more about the history and architecture of Mt. St. Michel than I could have learned in a year of library research. Listening to his lecture, I thought I began to understand the devotion of the saints. For the next hour we trailed Pierre through the cool of enormous vaulted rooms, carefully pocketing words like "Romanesque" and "flying buttresses." The structure of the abbey, he explained, reflected the social and ideological hierarchy of the Middle Ages. Its lowest level, housing the kitchens, refectory, and dormitories for lower-class pilgrims, reflected the body; the middle floor, containing the meeting house, library, scriptorium, and rooms for noble guests, corresponded to the educated mind, and the highest level, the chapel itself, represented the spirit. He didn't mention the village.

Outside we stared up at the walls in silence. The sense of quiet propriety was infectious. Finally, Kika said, "Why is it we're moved to make these places for some idea of God, but we don't make them for each other?"

And what would it be like if we did?

The true story of the abbey, Pierre had said earlier, was one of money and of power. He was talking about the shifting allegiances of the abbots during times of war, playing duke against king to benefit the abbey, but clearly it was all still true. In every way, this monastery, beautiful as it is, embodies the power structure of its times; money and power were still playing out the building's destiny, along with that of everyone who passed through it. Given that, I have to wonder, what is it possible to make for one another, even if we're moved to do so?

But then again, everything I've seen has shown me that the only way to escape those twin gods is by working for and with each other. This off-balance society is centered on climbing, reaching over and past one another; whether we're reaching toward a god of religion or of money is irrelevant. It's always just beyond us, just at the top. But what we build for each other starts at the bottom, in the village, in the details of our own imperfect bodies and uncertain lives. All the squats, all the *centros sociales*, all the houses and doors and hearts opened for us as we travel . . . every opening has felt like a step away from moneyandpower, a step into the something that we build for each other. Even when they seem flawed or faltering, these are living relics, the details that prove you can make a way to live wholly, even without the balance of money and power on your side. Throw in with us, they say, see what we can make together? You don't even have to climb your way to the top, you're already there.

letters

Pontourson is a town so small I still haven't found it on any map. We were only there because it happened to lie in a fork of the road; we were going one way and our ride was going the other.

As we stood in the center of town, an expectant kind of sadness colored everything around us. The last light of the day gleamed back from only the highest windows, the toll of church bells slowly filled the empty square. Like almost every dusk of the past four weeks, we were looking for a place to sleep; only tonight, for the first time, we could feel the end of summer coming toward us, the probability of long rain hanging in the heavy clouds. "Kika," I sighed, "I wish we had a home, just for tonight."

At first glance there was nothing unusual about the deserted house at 32 Avenue St. Michel, since Pontourson's sagging economy had left it with nearly as many abandoned buildings as occupied ones. A faded sign, "*A Vendre,*" probably years old, hung over the doorway, crooked shutters held back the empty rooms, vines were taking root in the crumbling mortar. And the front door, barely covered by cracked white paint, was held closed by only a thin scrap of wire that untwisted easily in my hand.

Welcome home. For a few days, anyway.

I woke up to sunlight streaming dusty through the open window, casting a net of vine-shadows across the floorboards. The night before, we'd had no chance to explore our hideout, but one look in the daylight was enough to reveal the whole house as a treasure box. Kika was already up, prowling curiously around the room. She called me over to examine the thick layer of old letters and papers that covered the closet floor and spilled out into the bedroom. They were mostly personal letters, addressed to 'Mami et Papa' or 'Grandmère LaRouche.' Some had been sent here, to Avenue St. Michel, and others had apparently been moved from a former house in another town. I was surprised that none of them had the usual worn edges of cherished letters, read a dozen times before they were boxed and tucked away.

"Chère Grandmère et Grandpère," I read aloud to Kika. "Sorry it has taken me so long to write. My new job is wonderful but I'm so very busy. Michelle is also busy with the twins . . . Sorry we couldn't come last week, we just had so much work on the house . . . Jacqueline is working hard at school, she's busy learning English . . ."

All the letters read this way; everyone was busy, everyone was working, they never had time or much to say, sorry, sorry, sorry. The dates on the letter head spanned maybe fifteen years, and their contents didn't vary much. Jacqueline grew up and stayed busy. The letters never got longer than a page. Not much to make them worth reading over and over again; but if that's all the contact you're getting from the people you love, you might want to hold on to them, just in case.

"Strange things to leave behind, don't you think?" Kika asked. She peered into one of the other cartons piled in front of fireplace and drew out an old-fashioned satin nightie. "This box is full of old clothes. They must have belonged to that woman, the grandmother." I could tell she was trying to piece the abandoned fragments into a story. "I bet her husband outlived her, and when he moved away he couldn't stand to go through all her favorite things, so he just left the whole box." As Kika held up lovely old slips and nightgowns and sweaters in a small parade of personal history, I could see the vanished woman's body taking shape, changing through the years.

We spent the whole morning raking our fingers through the remnants of the woman's home, imagining her life there. Kika, dressed in a long pink housecoat from the box, spun

a vision of Grandmère's life. Her voice was distant as she talked, her eyes focused behind me. Only the details mattered: This was the robe the woman had worn in the morning when she went to get the mail, when she sat drinking coffee, reading her son's short letters. This was the corner where her wide, comfortable bed had been; how she loved her afternoons alone, resting in the late-day light. This canvas was a painting of her husband's, she was the model: dark hair, red ribbon, white skin.

Dressed in her robe, trailing through the dust and shifting shadows, Kika was half herself and half the story; a little mad, a little ghostly. Wandering through the house, she examined various things she found; keys, broken clocks, small tea cups, lifting each one curiously between us. Everything she touched left its silhouette in the dust; it was as though each object was in two places at once, the positive figure and the negative, presence and the shape made by absence. She set each thing back exactly where it came from, leaving the dusty outlines undisturbed.

On the second day, I wandered into a small bar on the edge of town, Café Relax. It was empty except for a pair of young guys busy drinking their way into a good mood, mocking the tourists who passed through Pontourson on their way from Mt. St. Michel. "Pawnterrsun! Pawnterrsun!" they mimicked, imitating the British mispronunciation of *Pohntoursahn*. They roared with laughter while the bartender shook her head.

She and I took turns watching each other. As she sat disinterestedly reading a novel, her head kept turning to meet my eyes in the mirror. One hand unconsciously drifted up to tuck stray pieces of her messy blond chignon behind her ear, the peculiar way pieces of our body seem to move of their own volition. Finally she came over to where I sat writing and pointed at my notebook.

"You're a writer?" I nodded. "A novelist?"

Her eyes lit up hopefully, but her interest vanished

when I laughed and said, "Only letters home, unfortunately." Disappointed, she disappeared back into the book
she'd come from.

Letters home. Was that where I was writing back to?
When I left Olympia I thought I was taking home with me.
Like every other time I moved away, I was careful not to
leave behind anything I'd need in the future. Just in case. I
thought I could condense home to a few cubic feet I stowed
on the space of my back, could build a home from outer motion and inner fire. I know it's not keys to a nearby storage
unit that make a place home and it's only the bits of my heart
left on loan that are worth going back for. But is home the
place you come back to when you're full, or is it where you go
to be filled up again?

For the moment, "home" sounded like the delapidated
house where Kika was waiting for me. True, in most homes,
you don't have to hang heavy blankets over the windows to
hide the light, or speak constantly in low whispers, or peer
cautiously down the street before coming or going. But for
all its strangenesses, it was home for the same reason as the
places I sent my letters. No matter how I came back, full of
hope or desperate to be filled, someone I loved was waiting
there, holding a space for me.

✦✦ street rat dreamers

Being a dreamer doesn't always look like shine and stardust. Sometimes it just looks like dust, and I get tired of living this street rat life. Tired of being stared at on the sidewalks and hovered over in the stores, tired of being grabbed by the neck or the arm and shoved out of cafes where I'm trying to sneak into the restrooms to fill up our water bottles.

I know it happens because I'm dirty, because I carry my life on my back and have no apparent home or gender. It happens because I look like one of society's failed, and collectively we are terrified of both failure and the failed. In our culture of fear, we learn that the formulas for success and safety are one and the same. There are no alternate formulas, at least not ones that we can trust. So we mirror each other, policing the reflections for any aberrations.

My street rat life is a choice for me. I may re-enter that less deviant world any time I want. I can use my privilege to buy back respect from the same people who right now lock me out of it. All the keys to those doors are for sale. So why am I living in self-imposed exile?

Because you get what you pay for. Pay a lot and you get an expensive life. Take what's free, and you get freedom. On most people's terms this trip wouldn't have been possible. No, we didn't have money for the youth hostels, but who would've told us to keep dancing if we hadn't gone to Verottu Krottu? And if we'd taken the bus, we would've missed Pontourson. No cemetery picnics to be found in the formula for success. No cheap bread and stolen chocolate on the menu.

But off the map and beyond the borders of fear, there are other formulas. Abandoned houses - permission = free shelter and adventure. Rain + covered doorways = gratitude. Soon it's obvious that what you thought was flat actually has an underside, an edge, a core. That the mirrors you grew up with are as warped as the ones in the funhouse, and there's no going back to them. There's either giving up, or going on. One way cynicism, the other, dreams.

Even though I chose it, sometimes I resent my fork of the road, like when bathroom doors get slammed on me and I'm limping through the city in search of a bush. Cynically, I think: no wonder the cities all smell like piss, only the rich are allowed to urinate. I snarl at the inequities, I hiss at blatant stares, I drop my overalls and vow to quit dreaming.

But I can't. Even snarling, even hissing and cursing, I am reminded that there are angels everywhere. Angels choosing to sow the stars back into the dust. Angels inside the system, not just out, like Jan who picked us up yesterday, and drove miles out of his way to leave us at a good spot.

"Here's my phone number," he said after wishing us good luck, "so if you don't get a ride, you have a place to stay tonight."

Earlier, when Hibickina asked him what he would do if he didn't have to work his computer job, he had sighed and gazed out the window, past the asphalt to the water.

"I'd sail," he said. "I'd sail all the time."

"Dreamers stuck behind computers," Hibickina and I murmured half-sadly to each other later.

And then this morning, as we sat propped against the warmth of a brick restaurant wall, the proprietor came out and suggested that we come inside where there were tables. So we'd be more comfortable, no need to buy anything. Pleased, we ordered coffee anyway, and as we dug out our change he told us to pay only what we could.

". . . and that will be plenty," he smiled.

It is the nectar of the angel world that feeds the travelers on the road of dreams. We sustain each other, even when our equations vary. We're all angles of the thing that once looked flat. We bring its body to life. As it fleshes out, forms ridges, tests edges, bares a hidden belly and a beating heart at its core, the thing that once looked flat is recognizable as the other world we are creating. We make it home for each other. We open its doors when we offer kindnesses and we pass through those doors when we say yes. We make windows when we tell the stories.

1 september

if my dreaming makes me blind sometimes in this world, what else do i see for it?

i know that everywhere we go, there is another world within, beneath, outside & under. i see it in the houses that look like maybe they are or were or will be occupied, liberated. in the fading graffiti, "vivre ou mourir, c'est de nous à choisir." live or die, it's our choice to make. tiny whip lashes not even noticeable on the skin of this reality but to me sure signs that something is stirring beneath the surface. something that spells resistance. it's the signature of a second world, where we scramble desperately, joyfully, painfully to find another way. where we squat houses in defiance of the wage-slave cycle, plant our palms together in a refusal to be torn apart. where we've seeded wildflowers in all the empty broken spaces of the empty broken cities & our stories don't get lost in the traffic of growing older.

"you are dreaming!" liliane said to us & i thought yes, exactly, that is what we do, you know, being witches, being lovers, being poets & adventurers. we are dreaming this very moment, and so are you as a matter of fact. why not enjoy it? look down at your hands, remember you're dreaming & make it look how you want it to look, feel how you want it to feel. after all, the worlds we know are only made by dreamers.

downing the drawbridge

It wasn't exactly being homesick; really it was more like being lovesick. When Hibickina was reminded of a particular friend, her face would get all soft, and she'd say, "ohhhhh . . . Kika, I *miss* them." Or I'd have some experience which would suddenly give me insight into one of the people I adored, and a rush of fresh love would come scooting through my veins. But although we regularly composed epic letters professing our affections, they rarely got written down, much less sent off to the people we loved. Instead, the characters from our own histories remained a living conversation between us. We made memory collages from bits of their advice, from their tattoos and their libraries, their witchy kitchen shelves and dance club bedrooms. We arranged their revolutionary genius in mandalas of endearing idiosyncracies and sent our messages for them with the moon.

Road life meant living in whatever patches of love we could borrow: gardens in unlikely spots, alley cats with skinny purrs, bright liberation graffiti celebrating the walls, and good conversations on the stoops of new friends. We were sweet on the past, and pleased with the present. Soon the two would be bridged. Our friend Maegan was coming from Olympia to travel with us for a month. We were supposed to meet her at a cathedral in northern France.

Hibickina and I got to Cathedral St. Pierre early. It was huge, piercing the sky with spiky Gothic spires, catching the light in stained glass stars, guarded by gargoyles. We made a picnic while we waited; cheap bread, purple garlic, stolen chocolate. Given the menu and the scenery, it could've been any day of our wayward journey, but it wasn't. The world we were in was about to intersect with the one we'd come from.

I was airport-nervous, trying to act casual about being reconciled with someone I'm crazy about, but getting up every five minutes to check the path of arrival. On my seventeenth "walk," I finally saw her coming down the street. Easy confident stride, a charcoal shadow cutting sharp through the slow blurry crowd, the sun flashing in her auburn hair. Tight black pants and sexy dark-framed glasses, big old dusty brown boots. She looked like a raven who had recently flown out of an enchanted attic library. I could almost see bits of aged brown pages crumbling in her footsteps like confetti, and it seemed like she was stepping out from history and into the afternoon as I ran to meet her. Then that familiar wooly smell of her sweater mixed up with soap, her soft voice real in my ear, her gathering arms around me.

We sat on the steps trading stories, sometimes spilling fast over each others' words, hurried catching up; other times slow awkward questions and jutting spaces between us. This is how it always is, I thought, just because I've thought about Maegan so much, just because I've shared so much with her inside myself doesn't mean it's all immediately transmittable. I've been walking on one side of the river, she's been on the other. From our own shores we can see each other's castle, still standing sturdy, still lit up, but when it's time to cross back over that watery passage of space and time, it takes a while to get the drawbridge working smoothly. When it first comes down there's a lot of sticking and creaking.

Shortly after the close of dusk I left Maegan and Hibickina beneath the shadows of the gargoyles, and went to case out an abandoned house where we were hoping to sleep. My mind was a loud jangle of questions, the disconcertion of meeting up with your own past after you've been gone from it for a while. I was always afraid that the doors would close on me when I left, that I would return home and find no room saved for me inside.

Silence lay thick over the small dark street. The familiar ritual of secrecy comforted me. I loved the chase of my heart in my chest, the hunt for the next stolen treasure-chest home, this game of opening forbidden doors with shrewdness and skill. I pulled myself up over the wall with muscles

that felt solid, surer than the whirring conversation in my brain. When I jumped down, my dependable feet greeted the ground with the same quiet thump as always. My own pulse filled the empty space of night.

Entering the house was easy. I stood still and looked around. Slits of moonlight fell through the roof, a skeleton of rickety beams scabbed with rotting shingles and propped up by leaning wooden poles. I had wanted to bring back good news for my friends, I had wanted to unearth a secret abandoned palace in celebration of downing the drawbridge, but the lumpy dirt floors and dangerously angled walls offered no better shelter than the nearest park. So I crossed back over the sagging threshold of somebody else's long forgotten history and headed back to where my own was waiting for me, live and in the present, saving my spot for me on the steps of Cathedral St. Pierre. It was still warm when I got back.

——innate——resistance——

Suresh was an angel in a business suit. He stopped in the middle of the highway to make room for the three of us in his crowded sedan. "So," he said smoothly as he maneuvered back into the flow of traffic, "you're travelers headed where? Ah, Prague. I suppose you know, then, about the demonstrations happening there next month?"

Supposedly, the cardinal rule of getting on with strangers as you hitchhike is: *Don't talk politics.* You are trapped in their moving vehicle, after all, and you're likely to end up with an earful from some guy who's decided you're a prime audience for his reactionary rant, and who has absolutely no intention of letting you get a word in edgewise. Especially if you're female. Nonetheless, I've broken that magic rule in almost every car I've climbed into. By now I should know better than to expect all businessmen to fall into my stereotypes; I've met so many anarchist assholes and so many apolitical angels I ought to have learned to wait before I try to fit people neatly into my assumptions. All the same, at Suresh's opening comment my stomach sank in anticipation of yet another lecture about the futility of activism, the ignorance of anticapitalists, and the all-round impracticality of dreaming.

But Suresh paid attention to each word as the three of us slowly began to talk about our own politics. Finally, he said, "I think it's clear to many of us that something is missing from our lives. The numbers go up in the stock market, in the standard of living, the rates of unemployment go down, but clearly our lives are not getting better. I don't have time for this or that, we say—but fifty, even thirty-five years ago you wouldn't have heard that in Eastern Europe, for example. Everyone had time for their lives. Now . . . something is gone and there doesn't seem to be a way to get it back. But no one knows who to blame, who's accountable."

"Maybe that's part of the point of these protests," Maegan countered. "Not to make it so the new enemy is the head of the IMF or the WTO, but so there can be something real to focus our anger on, something that makes it possible for people to try to look at the systems that are really behind what we're talking about."

"Perhaps. But I doubt very much that any kind of real social movement is possible anymore. The thing is that we're just too behaved, we're all groomed to be very, very obedient. You see all these dissident theories being published all over the place, but who's paying attention? We're free to talk about change all we like, but we're equally conditioned not to respond, to even our own ideas. Those people who claim to be fighting for radical change—they claim success when they enter negotiations with their opponents, but that isn't change. It's just a different round of obedience."

A sticky silence fell. Kika and Maegan both looked out the windows, chewing on their own thoughts. I shook my head impatiently at the highway. I don't have time for his kind of hopeless pragmatism, I thought, I haven't got enough certainty to withstand the sense of futility, it slides too easily into nihilism. I'm tired of being told that the Last Real Social

Movement ended in Paris '68, or Berkeley '69, Poland '81, or wherever, just like I'm sick of being written off because I look young, because I'm a girl, because I talk about wings and dreams and poetry. I've been standing guard vigilantly on top of a fortress of possibility, trying desperately to shoot arrows with dream-messages attached straight into the hearts of everyone who crosses my path. Now my arms are getting tired, and if I listen long enough to everyone trying to shout me down eventually I'll just take their advice and throw myself off the parapet. Best to leave this argument to Maegan and Kika and their kinder words, I thought, I'm too snappish to defend the politics of hope.

Suresh, watching me in the rearview mirror, smiled sagely. "I don't think it's entirely hopeless, though. For the last thirty years, in my own small ways I've been watching the world change. There are two places I've seen the most possibility to shift the course of things, even the course of history if you like." Oops. What was it I just said about waiting to leap into my assumptions? "The first is that, in certain places, there are cultures, smaller communities which are nearly impervious to any economic onslaught. In Southern Italy, for instance, where my wife comes from, and in some places in India, where I was born; it's impossible to make the lives of these people become wrapped around external systems of money and economic power. Their lives are elsewhere. And consequently their culture is so strong, resistance is innate.

"And the second—well, let me give you an example. This was years ago, when I worked in the steel industry for a large firm; as a vice president I was told to lay off first three hundred, then all six hundred workers at one particular plant. The company wasn't even in a bad position, really, but the profit margins could have been higher. In any case, I knew it was unnecessary, there were other solutions, though of course if I refused to make the firings I would lose my job." He smiled mischievously as he said this, as though deliberately losing one's extremely well-paid upper-management position were a slightly daring prank rather than fodder for a midlife crisis.

"I didn't refuse outright; instead I offered to buy the plant. Of course it was impossible and in the end I was fired, but it forced the company to acknowledge that the plant was still profitable, and it could no longer simply be shut down."

Kika nodded vigorously. "*That's* how changes happen, I think we start to realize that we aren't only cogs in the wheels of some machine that just grinds on and on no matter what we do. Even though they seem so removed from us, ultimately none of these systems work without our participation. We *are* that machine, in ones and twos and small groups and hundreds, and that means we're the ones who can make the cracks in it. That's where my biggest hope is, the possibility of refusing to participate in our own powerlessness. What makes it so hard, though, at least in the States—is that we've got such thick illusions about our choices; it's like you said before, we're conditioned not to act, and that's constantly reinforced by the idea that there's only just a few narrow possibilities in the first place. That's how we start making those cracks, by making new possibilities."

Suresh agreed. "Once you begin to have some insight into the way things are actually moving . . . once you open your eyes and you see the need for change, you either become a wise person, you turn inward and look for answers there, or else you become a revolutionary."

He laughed. "Or maybe you do both, if you have time."

Suddenly I thought understood how it was that Suresh could speak at once with such detachment that it sounded like hopelessness, and then go on to talk about the potential for change with optimism that bordered on certainty. I thought about our friend back in Olympia who always says, "Revolution is more fun than monopoly." For Suresh, this was all a game, but with real human players. For him, hope wasn't something you had to defend vigorously, it just *was*; hope was innate, the way he'd described resistance. And in fact the two come from the same place.

Resistance is crushed by conquering hope, by convincing us that either there's nothing better to work for, or else that it can never be achieved. But Suresh had already disproved that in his life. Whether it happens with 50,000 other people in the streets of Seattle or between the walls of an all-girl squat, whether it comes through small groups or a massive social movement—Suresh had reminded me that change is possible, more is possible. When we divide our resistance from our hope, we back ourselves into a corner and we lose both; but when we allow ourselves the freedom to imagine more, when we help each other insist that change is possible, that's when we have the strength to create it. Sometimes, more hope is the best thing you can hope for.

street sign liberated outside
le park, normandie.

shelter

Olivier jangled his keys in his palm as he led us toward his house. "It's just a *pied á terre*," he warned for the second time. "I'm still fixing it up, so it's a mess. No hot water, no furniture, but you're welcome to stay for a few days."

When we'd first climbed into his car, a thousand years ago on the grimy freeway, Olivier had told us, "The people in Liège are the nicest in the world. I've traveled all over but I keep coming back here because they're so good. You'll see." I smiled politely and kept my thoughts to myself. We'd learned that angels were few and far between; if there actually were an entire city full of them it would probably lift itself off the map and disappear forever, it wouldn't stick around in a maze of grey canals halfway between Brussels and the German border. At least, that was what we thought before Olivier drove us into the city center, led us by hand to the best waffle place in town, then returned promptly one hour later to pick us up again. This time, he had his spare keys in hand. Our chivalrous chauffeur in a dirty red hatchback, he delivered us to his empty flat, all the while saying, "It's nothing, it's nothing."

"This is my street." Olivier pointed to a tall wooden fence. As he reached for the handle, the gate swung open in front of us and a tall woman emerged from the cool bower of a narrow cobblestone lane. She moved with steady unconscious grace, a poplar tree walking toward us, light catching in the leaves of her dark hair.

"Ah, *ma voisine*, Isabelle!" Olivier cried. They spoke briefly, and Isabelle smiled deeply at each of us. She left us with an invitation to come next door to her flat for hot showers or anything else we needed, and wouldn't we stop by at sunset for a drink? Like Olivier, she also said, *"De rien, de rien."* Is this what's meant by kindness, welling up effortlessly, thoughtlessly? It's nothing, it's nothing. Maybe I hadn't known kindness before.

We followed Olivier into the courtyard. The cobble-stoned alley was bordered on one side by a row of brightly painted doors, and on the other by a tall wooden fence covered in a profusion of morning glories and ivy. Green things grew everywhere—lavender and mint exploded out of window boxes, geraniums overflowed their hanging baskets, strawberries vined up the legs of the wrought iron benches, and wicker chairs waited patiently outside each flat. Several round cats dozed in patches of sun, oblivious to the white butterflies flickering over their heads. We'd walked only five minutes from the bright rush of downtown Liège and some-how we'd arrived in a fairy tale.

When I was a little girl, I believed in magic. Not the fantasy kind, grey-bearded wizards and lightning bolts shooting from my fingertips; I knew real magic, the kind you feel through your entire body, the whole world collapsed in your chest and the moon lodged in your throat like a song. I saw fairies on a hillside, sat in the garden and talked with the trees, stepped across the fork of three streams and crossed into a bower of branches that sang to me while I cried. At night the moon drew herself down through the window, a blue-white woman hanging over me as I slept. As I grew older, though, I got lost from magic. I was repeatedly assured that the fairies were only insects shining in a shaft of light, the songs of trees were only wind, and all the secret worlds I found were imagined and irrelevant. After a while I went along with this version of events. Who has time for magic when you've got a meeting to go to?

But I was always waiting for it to come back to me. Somewhere in my heart I carved out a space with a tarnished spoon, I tacked up a sign that said 'love and freedom spo-ken here' and I waited for magic to creep back in. I waited through pages of endless books, through slow hands of innu-merable clocks, thousands of sunsets and uncountable con-stellations. I waded through my days and when I closed my eyes at night I was still waiting for magic to happen to me. I thought it would curl up toward me, faint and irresistible like incense smoke; I expected it to appear like mushrooms springing out of loamy earth, rich and musty, born from what's already long dead.

If you'd asked, I probably wouldn't have guessed magic would finally find me in a narrow alley somewhere in eastern Belgium, tired and dirty and with nothing between me and an unfamiliar city but a rickety wooden gate. But there it was when I walked through the gate of Cour Moreau, something in the stillness between the vines, saying quietly, *this is magic, magic is possible here.*

Sunset came and hung bars of long gold light across the alley. The morning glories curled in on themselves for the night and one by one the drowsy cats began to rouse themselves and slink off into the evening streets. Kika, Maegan and I trailed the shadows two doors down to Isabelle's house, where she introduced us to another neighbor, Marie-Jean, who quickly became our translator. We sat talking slowly, drinking pale Belgian beer and nibbling fresh grapes, breathing in the sky as it grew purple. Isabelle and Marie-Jean questioned us about our travels, both sets of eyes lively and curious. These were not the distant queries of one stranger to another: So how has your trip been, What museums did you visit, Oh isn't that hotel lovely? Their questions were real doorways, invitations to let loose the river of our stories, the world drawn in through our bodies, transformed in our hearts, pouring out through our words and our hands. We talked in rounds about angels in automobiles, rain storms and cathedrals, squats and scenes and punk boys.

"So you're traveling the alternative circuit, eh? Liège is small but it also has its own circuit." With the ease of women used to making their own maps, Isabelle and Marie-Jean sketched the outline of the second face of Liège, full of squatted secret cafés, experimental orchestras, public poetry,

open doors. Liège was full of experiments in saying yes. Of course, not all experiments are successful. For almost twenty years, Marie-Jean was telling us, she'd helped run a grass-roots women's center, Café des Femmes. "I left even before it closed, though. I'd started drinking again and my life eventually fell apart." As she talked I could see her heart hanging behind the thin veil of her eyes, sandpapered to softness by years of exploring, stumbling, picking herself up again to say yes to something new. "Finally I came here to Cour Moreau as I was putting things back together."

"This is a magic place, isn't it?" Isabelle smiled. "Before I lived here, I moved twenty-nine times in twenty-nine years—this is my first real house." I never would have guessed it from her cozy flat, a settled haven of rich warm colors, full of candlelight and soft shadows, safe refuge from even the coldest city shoulder.

"Before, I just traveled like you, I stayed with friends I met on the way. It's funny, you know, I was born in Belgium, but it's only coincidence that I live here now. I was always moving, from the time I was seventeen—from Italy to Spain, the Pyrenees, France . . . always looking for something, I guess. Then I came here and I met Mireille. She's the reason I stayed, really, she made it home."

The way Isabelle said *Home*, it became a weighted word—not cumbersome but tangible, something to be taken seriously and seriously loved. *Home*. It was still new for her, this way of staying put after so many years of motion. But somehow she made it sound like the best idea in the world.

It stormed the next day, coloring the sky with the same grey sheen as the canals, the pigeons, the tired leaning buildings downtown. Inside the alley, though, everything seemed to maintain its own bright color: lavender, green, brick red, vividly refusing to run together even in the downpour. We passed the afternoon in the warm shelter of Isabelle's flat, watching the watery shadows pour over the tile. There were no mirrors in her house and no clocks; Isabelle moved through the house singing with a grace that made it plain she kept her own time, saw her reflection clearly enough in the hearts around her. Somehow being there with her gave us license to do the same, to pass our time sipping tea, piecing together frames from our lives the way we watched Isabelle weave willow sticks and rushes into supple baskets, a family of witches laughing quietly. When Marie-Jean came home in the evening we settled into dinner in her dense kitchen, clustered over photos from her "theater days." Marie-Jean as Puck, as a mime, a warrior, costumed in all her realest faces, the ones most of us are busy hiding under the unified front that keeps out the world.

Finally, after all the dishes had been washed and stacked, we had to admit that morning was not far off. Nearly time for us to leave Cour Moreau for wider roads.

"Ah, girls," sighed Marie-Jean as we stood shadowed in her doorway. "You know, it gives me hope—I get to see now that there are still real travelers and dreamers out in the world. I almost thought those paths were done for twenty years ago, and now to see you building them all over again . . . Oh, I have such hopes. You'll follow your dreams all the way to the end," she said confidently.

Her eyes were heavy blue and shining like the moon woman who had watched over me when I was a girl. "Just use your heart to feel your way through what's in front of you and you'll never get lost."

As Kika and Maegan and I walked slowly back to our own little cottage at the end of the alley, I thought, *This is where magic is;* in the lines of our laughter and our stories, where we make a haven from what hurts us in the rest of the world, in the chance to turn our fears and disappointments into dreams. Where we touch each other, where we leave room to be touched; to say here, here are the wings of my heart, make a roof from it, make a shelter. *This* is magic, this is shelter, this gift we give each other.

⊙ accident prone ⊙

In the back of Geoff's parked semi, we all lay uneasy and awake, our eyes widened against the darkness. Wet branches slapped against the heavy doors. The freeway paralleled the truck stop, and road noise blended with the steady engine hum of resting refrigerated loads. We had rigged the doors so they couldn't be closed from the outside without waking us, and we spoke to each other in hushed tones.

"I just hate feeling like a target," Maegan whispered. It wasn't irrational; traveling female negates certain states of relaxation. The truck stop was full of leering international drivers, all male, most bored, many drunk. "Don't worry," Hibickina assured her, "Kika's knife is really sharp." The protective powers of my blade were an ongoing joke between us, but what she really meant was, *we're smart enough, we're sly enough, we're quick enough to avoid danger, see how we done so far? You're safe with us baby . . .*

But this was the first time we'd slept in a semi. Until now, summer had been our constant companion, meaning any darkened corner was a place to sleep, any hidden weedy hollow a potential bed. But Germany was a slate of cold rain and none of us had a tent, or much more warmth than what we were wearing. Geoff's offer had been our best option.

I hated feeling so guarded against him after all he'd done for us. It would've been stupid not to be paying absolute attention, but still, I was pretty convinced he was an angel. He'd picked us up that morning just after we'd crossed from Belgium into Germany, and said he could take us almost all the way to the Czech border. He was English, and we hadn't been driving more than an hour when he offered us tea and scones. From the cozy loft of his cab, we sipped the hot tea and watched the sleeting grey skyline.

"You haven't lived until you've eaten scones," he reported morosely, spreading thick strawberry jam. "At least, I couldn't live without them."

Everything he said was melancholic, a rhythmic Eeyore's monologue as we jounced through the German countryside, heavy rain streaking the broad windshield. Once we'd heard parts of his history, it wasn't hard to figure out why.

Geoff had been the youngest of a pack of children, and shortly after his birth his father disappeared. His mother gave them up to separate orphanages. His new world was empty of friends, much less saviors. An incredible ability to withdraw was his sole survival skill. But it made him an easy target for cruelty.

"Once, when I was about four or five, I wet the bed at the orphanage . . . as children do, you know. There were two women who were the foster mothers there, and one of them was called Mrs. Fordes. A right dragon, she was. When she saw I'd wet the bed, she went into a blind fury, and beat me in the face with a wooden-backed hairbrush. Broke my nose and my jaw, and gave me two black eyes. Had to keep me out of nursery school for nine weeks to hide the damage to my face. I used to disappear beneath a table when she came into the room.

"Sometimes I think that's why I'm shy of women. I wish I wasn't . . . Oftentimes I think I'd like to get married. I love children, that's why. When I see young children with their parents, especially lovely little girls, I rather think I'd like to have a little girl like that, and treat her well."

The low moony monotone barely rose above the sound of the engine. "It makes me sad, you know, when I read about the terrible things that happen to children. Sometimes it makes me feel I want to cry," he confessed. "I often think I ought to quit this job, so I could have a bit more of a social life, instead of driving for months on end. Twenty-eight years it's been. Perhaps if I was in one place, I could get married, and raise a family. I often dream about that. I often dream about having a happy life in the countryside. But maybe it's too late."

"I don't think so," I said. "Really I don't think it's ever too late to begin your dreams. I don't think there's some point in life when dreams stop being possible, or some age when you should stop dreaming. Especially in a world where your only alternatives are fear and submission."

"Or numbness," Maegan chimed in. "I don't think it's too late, either. I think you're lucky, because you know what you want. That makes it easier to start."

"And since you're getting more experienced all the time, it's easier to figure out the most direct route there."

"It's a rather small dream," he said shyly.

"It's your dream," Maegan responded softly.

I paged through Geoff's atlas while long silences lapsed comfortably around us. We grew drowsy with the warmth from the heater. Maegan curled up on the bed behind the seats, and Hibickina looked quietly out the window as we drew closer and closer to the Czech Republic. Every so often Geoff began another set of stories, all beginning with "once."

"Once I got in a truck wreck, a right nasty one. Truck went over the bridge, and the trailer fell on top of it. Broke my back, and stayed in a coma for 39 days. Spent six months in a hospital bed. I'm rather lucky, I suppose. Most people said I should have died."

"How did the truck go over the bridge? What happened?"

"A car was coming, passing another car. They were going much too fast. Bridge was right narrow. If I hadn't swerved, they would've run straight into me, and surely they would have died."

My throat felt mealy. "And the car? Did they see what happened to you? Did they stay?"

"Suppose they must've, how could you not notice a semi go over the bridge in front of you? But nobody stayed. When the ambulance came I had been there for hours." He spoke matter-of-factly, not a trace of bitterness at his misfortune.

"Well, that's not the only time I've had a tumble. Once I decided to learn to ride a motorcycle. I'd always wanted to know how. Fellow I was friends with had one, and one day we went up to a parking lot so I could get a lesson. It was all going rather well until it was time to stop. I confused the controls, and hit the gas instead of the brake. Unfortunately there was a twenty-foot embankment dropping off from the lot and I was headed straight for it.

"Ended up flying through the air and rolling over and over on the ground. Broke four ribs and only narrowly missed the spot where the motorcycle crashed down.

"I suppose you could say I'm accident prone," he finished, smiling sheepishly.

Later, all of us ate dinner together at a smoky table in the crowded trucking restaurant, making scant conversation through the clatter of silverware and the din of languages. After we ate, we warned him, we would probably be boring company, lost in our journals.

"It's all right," he said, excavating a small worn volume from his breast pocket. "I've got one too. I like to write a bit each day, take note of what I think is special. They're rather nice, diaries."

In the morning Geoff knocked carefully on the back door of the truck and when we opened it, he offered to make the rounds of the parking lot and ask all the eastbound truckers if they had room for three extra passengers.

"And I left some scones and cereal for you in the cab, if you'd like a bit of breakfast before you go."

When he returned with the good news of another ride, he handed me the atlas.

"You ought to keep it," he told me, "I can see you like geography, and I never was much good at it myself."

"Thanks, Geoff," I said, rolling it up and tucking it in my pack. He smiled his shy smile as I reached to give him a hug, and patted me awkwardly on the back.

"I'll miss having the three of you around," he said. "I've rather enjoyed your company. It might sound a bit sappy, but it's almost felt like having three daughters to look after.

"Keep in touch."

CROSSING

Not so very long ago, this border was as real as they come, a crossing from iron into steel. The legacy isn't entirely gone. So many elements of clichéd Cold War border crossing scenes were still in place, it was almost comic: looming stormy sky, fog in black-green hills, blocky cement buildings. Inside the closed glass booth, the guards slouched smoking hand-rolled cigarettes under drooping mustaches. They all wore their uniforms open over stained white undershirts, showing hairy chests and raw pink skin. Sharp-eyed border patrollers with angular faces paced the periphery, long leather coats snapping with each footstep. The only thing missing was the barbed-wire fence. But the scene shifted when we actually crossed; none of the vicious looking guards gave a damn about three very scruffy, vaguely suspicious Americans strolling across their border. They waved us across the painted white line with barely a glance at our passports.

When I crossed into the Czech Republic I was facing the new reality of an old dream. I stepped across a certain boundary of fear when I said goodbye to my steady life, filled my backpack and took off without a return ticket. To some people, that was no more than an easy, romantic gesture; my friend Goblin just shook his head and said, "Europe's not so scary." But it wasn't noble heroics I was after, that wasn't the point. I didn't decide to travel this way—with no map and no certainty and very little money, relying on strangers as much as myself—because it was bold or adventurous or even original. I just had to do it that way to get across the real border, which is the one in my own head and heart.

It helps to remember that borders are only invisible arbitrary lines. We've lived for so long with the idea of the border that it's become ingrained, and we've forgotten that it's only a construction. We painted those white lines ourselves and agreed to call them national boundaries, the same way that whatever the majority of people agree on we call 'reality.' But it's possible to depart from that paradigm and create a new one. Of course, practically speaking, you still have to navigate the dominant reality. Whether I believe in these constructed borders or not, I still have to cross them. It's the same with the ones I've created inside myself.

We all have our own borders. On one side is what's easy, what's known, what we've been told is true and have taken for granted; it's comfortable here, it's familiar. But the other side is wider than possibility, it's brilliant with potential, and it looks like our dreams, whatever they are. Maybe for you that means having a family or taking up sailing; maybe it's poetry in Prague or solitude in Barcelona; maybe it's learning how to really be close to someone. Big or small, these are not the "dreams" we've had handed to us, goodjob/bighouse/newcar—these are real dreams, real fragile fledgling dreams, which is why they're often so frightening. But they're *ours*, if we can find them and hold them, if we can catapult ourselves across whatever border of fear or doubt or tiredness seems to keep us from them. In the end, the only thing standing between each of us and what we most want, is ourselves. We're our own border guards. And sometimes the crossing is easier than expected.

gargoyles

We'd daydreamed all the way from the border to Prague as we watched the flat gold fields roll by. Goblin was there in the city, somewhere, and we hoped we'd find him that night and curl up comfortably on his floor; we imagined our way into a warm cozy flat with bowls of hot soup waiting for us. But as it turned out, Goblin's "address" was a tent in a field full of goats somewhere on the edge of the city, and it was now long past dark, much too late to find him that night. In the end, we crept into the depths of an untended office building and made our own camp in its quiet basement.

Maegan curled up to sleep in a corner while Kika and I stood guard, writing in our journals. Ostensibly, anyway; in fact I was only hunched motionless over its pages listening to the wheels turn in my brain and my heart pound a nervous, tired rhythm. Kika looked over at me curiously.

"We're gargoyles!" she hissed happily. "We're the gargoyles in the basement of the library."

I wondered briefly what gargoyles would be doing in the basement, although in Prague I wouldn't really be surprised to find them anywhere. In the scant hour we'd spent out in the city, I'd already seen their stone silhouettes everywhere. There seemed to be an abundance of statues on every street corner: human figures on pedestals and rooftops, fantastic faces locked into the walls, dragons and fierce medusas guarding elaborate windows. Heroes and martyrs and saints, meant to commemorate stories, but lost now in the rush of speeded-up history.

"Do you know what gargoyles are about?" I asked Kika. "The usual mythology is that they're meant to chase away malicious spirits. But there's an alternate version that says gargoyles all used to be human, before they kept one secret too many locked inside themselves and just turned to stone." I believe it; secrets are only the silent face of fear, after all, and I know too well the feeling of granite that grows from my throat down to my toes.

She thought for a minute. "Well, let's not turn to stone, then. Tell me a secret."

A month before, I would have said something banal but vaguely interesting, I would have dredged up some easy story I hadn't told her yet. But it's difficult to wear your usual stony mask around someone who's watched you turn inside out in the course of a few weeks. I looked up at the shadows in the dusty corners and imagined myself perched motionless on the same rafter for a hundred years.

"I'm terrified, Kika. Do you remember how we said, a million miles away on that road outside Foix, how different we felt? It's like now I'm suddenly the same again, I can feel all this fear welling up in my chest, the way I haven't felt since I left the States. What if I'm wrong and everyone who's told me I'm crazy is right? What if I can never make sense of this weird bony language and Goblin doesn't love me anymore and I just keep getting lost in the curvey streets? Dreams are so precarious, Kika, and really that's all I've got. What if just having the dreams isn't enough to change anything and I'm not smart enough or brave enough or strong enough to ever really make them real?"

"Hibickina." I thought I heard leathery wings unfolding as Kika stood and walked over to me. She wrapped her arms around me and said firmly, "Listen. Didn't we just come across two continents writing on the walls *love is freedom*? Our chains rusted and we replaced them with keys. We made it here on a map made of dreams and stories, we made our own maps and our own stories. This is life, Hibby, it doesn't stop coming on full force. Don't let a little fear get in the way of your dreams coming on that strong, too."

I looked down from my corner and into her eyes. Even in the shadows they were lit up from the inside, fiery with Kali-love and Medusa-wisdom.

I remembered something Goblin had written to me years before: "Life means always questioning, always asking Why? *Why?* Every moment of the day." Sitting there curled in Kika's fierce love and strong arms, I thought, yes, life means turning the questions on your own ideas, not just everybody else's; but it also means leaving room between the question marks to make answers with the people you love. Answers that look like dreams, answers that sound like wings before they turn to stone.

arrival

Before I left the States I'd been told about a squat here, an old fort in the middle of a gigantic park, and Hibickina and I had imagined it as her new home. It sounded like a good way to spend the dark winter: the long chill of nights warmed by strong walls around a strong community, hot coffee, storytelling by the falling fireplace. Other dreamers living in layers of moth-eaten sweaters.

Or at least a better place to stay than this basement, I thought, after our two measly hours of sleep that first night in Prague. Hibickina, Maegan and I tiptoed back up several flights of stairs to ground level, striding quick and determined past the cleaning lady who almost dropped her broom and did drop her jaw at the sight of three near-apparitions with bleary eyes and ratty packs. Out the door we fled into the 6 a.m. workday streets, laughing despite ourselves, at ourselves, at the idea of dreaming at all. Hibickina set off to search out Goblin, disappearing into a sea of briefcases. Maegan and I were supposed to find the squat.

We stumbled through the maze of cobblestones, our bodies heavy with unslept sleep, bumping into coppered angels who smiled their condolences but offered no salvation. Jesters leered from above heavy wooden doorways, goddesses drowsed on parapets, fountains spat tiny watersongs in small plazas. From a distance I saw a hooded iron figure. A flush of birds rose from its cloak as we neared and I looked into its face but the face wasn't there. Inside the hood was only empty black space. The form was human but the cloak held its shape by iron alone.

High up, cathedral spires beckoned the sky in a profusion of gilded fingers, crumbling bell towers sounded weary chimes. Stone lions guarded even the lampposts and never before had I been in a city where there was room for art like there was here, where the works of the imagination didn't stop with a park or a plaza or even a time but spread throughout centuries and an entire city. Every beast from Noah's ark, every divinity from ancient Greece was snared in stone, prisoners and mythical tutelars of this urban Garden of Eden. The parks were yellow and red with September apples.

We found Ladronka in the afternoon, a dismal fortress where silent punk boys sat indoors in still rows, smoking and coughing, the late-summer sunshine floating hazy over gritty mattresses and the steady beat of drag, cough, drag, cough. Being female we were, as usual, invisible. The walls were covered with male signatures, *Jiri was here, Ladronka Rocks 2/10/98, FUCK capitalismo!!! Marselo de Madrid*. Sure you can stay for one night only and no we have absolutely no interest in speaking to you. We are very busy. Smoking.

None of us had slept more than a few hours in several days by the time we returned to Ladronka late that night, our tram circled the entire city twice before we realized we had fallen asleep with our dry eyes open. I didn't notice when mine finally closed, I was dreaming about Verottu Krottu, about Cour Demain and Kasa and Keimada wondering if Hibickina could salvage the life she wanted for herself here.

In the morning I woke to the crustiest foot I'd ever seen poking out of a nearby blanket, years of black sludge walled between the toes, the talon-like nails yellowed and broken, colonies of fungus so dark at first I thought it was wearing a shoe. Its owner was still asleep. As we were leaving, the only person who spoke to us was the one other woman there. When we were back outside, crossing over the grassy expanse of park, I looked at Hibickina, expecting a critical analysis on gender roles in squat culture or at least an update on how it felt to face her dreams. Instead she said, "Did you see that *foot?*"

Homeless. Goblin lived with the goats, Ladronka was a stupid scene, and the nights were getting cold. Where to go? Our days blurred into one long search. We fed ourselves into the whirling machine of the subway, where the rows of washed out fluorescent-lit faces looked thwarted, half-divinities from the city of angels sitting impotent on metro seats, unable to use their magnificent powers of creation. That absolute, instinctual drive to create had been harnessed and tamed by capitalism, and before capitalism by communism, and always by somebody else's work. Dreams lost in the vacuum of the timecard.

Still, the ghost of creative glory was greywashed over the motionless habit-worn faces, too innate to ever disappear completely. It simply mutates when it is not expressed; turns violent and perverse; dries up or withers into apathy; leaves us grieving over our own wasted lives even as we live them. There in the electric carriages of emptiness, people were connected by underground tunnels passing beneath jittering streets, but never by each other. Strangers avoided each other's every gaze, or occasionally, reached into eyes to scoop out anything unguarded. Scoop it out, throw it away like a used ticket. Stamp and dismiss.

Complacency, the collectively learned rhythm. Gone the natural human rhythms, gone the time for play, replaced now by sequences of clockwork time. The three of us were right in the middle of it. An entire world had forgotten how much they once loved recess and in the midst of city life this amnesia was contagious. Survival mode had been far more romantic on the road. We were spat from line to line, washed upstream on the mountainous escalators, delivered from metro to tram until we were dumped dizzy back on the streets. Still searching.

"You might need time to nurse the wounds of your dreams," I said to Hibickina one day in the street. "This is not what you expected but anything you are ready to love is lovable, even it it's scarred or fucked-up or broken. These are still good and worthy dreams."

It was more of a prayer than consolation, as we passed empty building after squattable empty building in the streets but learned how harsh squatting regulations are in Prague, how short-lived and few the squats. As we sidelined the political community, and failed our own attempts to integrate ourselves in ways we believed in. Days passed, and for the first time in any city, the only friends we had were each other. It was a prayer for all the dreams with bruises or sore muscles or open cuts from the places where they'd crashed into the solid walls of reality.

It was Jana and Hansa who finally saved us. Goblin suddenly remembered that he had friends here, "Oh I know someone you can maybe stay with," he said, after we'd been searching for days, in the surprised tone Goblin gets when he remembers something offhand which coincidentally is a perfect solution for the current dilemma.

Hibickina and Maegan and I were miserable and desperate, frustrated that we couldn't create what we needed for ourselves, that magic didn't seem to work here. We were reluctant to impose on people who didn't know us and who actually didn't even know Goblin very well and who weren't offering something of their own volition. But in the end we followed Goblin up a quiet street to an old apartment building where he rang a bell that read Vales.

Jana and Hansa took us in, put on some tea which, Hansa said, they'd grown and harvested at their family's country cottage. We sat awkwardly in their clean living room, sipping the hot fragrant tea, wondering what these people could possibly be thinking of three very dirty and somewhat scary-looking foreigners who had been presumptuous enough to show up on their doorstep. But they weren't thinking, they were asking, leaving room for us to explain ourselves. Why were we here in Prague? What would we do here? They asked if we'd come for the anticapitalism protests and I felt vaguely uncomfortable, unenthused about the prospect of a political conversation which might put us at odds. But while I would have been happy to listen to their story without divulging my own, Maegan answered candidly, giving voice to the questioning that was being done by herself, Hibickina and I: how it was that each of us wanted to put our radical politics into daily action. With Maegan being so open there was no way I could be closed. Gingerly I joined the conversation.

Jana and Hansa listened carefully to what all three of us had to say, responding to our critique of capitalism with a critique of the communism under which they were raised. We discussed the politics of hope from both angles and in the morning, Jana caught us in the kitchen with the sun in her eyes.

"Girls," she said, "please stay here. Please stay here with Hansa and I in our flat until you find a place to stay. We've been up late talking about you, and we've been saying how inspiring was our conversation, and I think we could learn so much from each other because we are so different, and still so the same. Will you stay?"

We stayed.

The next night Jana and I sat whispering in the kitchen by candlelight after everyone else had gone to bed.

"It's so simple," she said. "Really Kika, it's simple: to love yourself and to love others, to not damage yourself or others. I don't know why we make it so complicated."

Somehow it did seem simple when Jana said it. It still seems simple when I sit across from her by candlelight, sipping hot tea out of one of her huge mugs, or when I walk through the night with her while she does imitations of George Bush. *"Since everyone loves America, and wants to be like us,"* she intones, *"it's our duty to give other countries that opportunity . . ."* I'm laughing on the Charles bridge, clutching my stomach at her near-perfect English and dead-on imitation of Bush's presidential platform. "How stupid," Jana says. "Why would we want to be like America? We have our own culture, own language, our own ideas. I don't want to be like America."

I don't want to be like America either, not that part of America anyway. I don't want to be like anything that tries to get me to buy my dreams instead of making them myself. I'd rather tend the wounds of my dreams when they crash into someone else's reality than give them up. I'd rather make maps of their scars and accept their ever-changing forms than buy into the huge, pre-packaged dream that's sold in the global supermarket. I don't want to learn the rhythm of complacency.

It isn't an easy undertaking to rebuild your world. It's habit for the juice of dreams to get wrung out in theory and cynical pragmatism, to be questioned and processed into a corner of silence or defeat. But when we live in our own worlds, worlds we have dreamed and created, worlds which sometimes surprise us, worlds we share and speak about loudly, resistance again becomes innate.

as much as i can hold.

When I find myself in this place of incontrovertible aliveness, when the world is on fire and I am with it—I think, I won't forget this, I won't be lost in the pettiness of the day-to-day, my own turmoil, I won't succumb to sorrow or inertia or fall prey to fear. None of it matters nearly as much as this joy, this knowing the beauty of each thing exactly as it is.

Recently I have begun to think, more realistically, I probably *will* forget this; I will be caught up in stuckness and I will be afraid, I will be numbed by the horror of everything around me and I will feel small and tired and lost. But this time I will try to remember a space beyond it. I will try to remember the boundless hope and consuming joy and know that it's still there, somewhere. Holding out behind a curtain of small terrors and a fog of futility is a fortress of uncontainable bliss waiting to be unleashed again in my heart and the world.

And I go on making small promises to myself in the meanwhile: I will walk every day in between the trees, I will make some celebration, I will love without fear, I will create beautiful things, I will be unafraid to fly, I will move and speak and live deliberately . . . My promises stretch out and out sometimes past the horizon of possibility, and often at the end of the day it seems I've never walked as far as I thought I could. I get discouraged and wake up tired in the morning. But I go on making promises, because the sunrise is so beautiful, and those three stars are still shining so brightly, and the birds are beginning to sing, you can hear them even over the whine of the highway. In spite of myself I feel the embers of hope and I think, well maybe I could make it just to the end of that road, after all. And I make myself some more promises, I call them dreams, and when night comes I don't let go of them, I congratulate myself on the ones that walked through the length of the day with me and tuck the rest of them in to carry me through tomorrow.

Occasionally I get disgusted with the whole process, I think *Ugh, Dreams and Promises and Possibilities*, where have you gotten me? Full of you but I'm still getting nowhere. Maybe you're only extra weight after all and reality is just about as much as I can hold. I vow to leave them all by the wayside and I pretend I don't notice it's only another promise I'm making. I try to drag myself through the rows of days, not getting distracted, not floating away. But what I notice (after a while of not noticing anything) is that I can't see much *except* dreams, and promises, and possibilities—only they're not mine, they're everyone else's, everyone who never bothered to get burdened by Reality. in the first place. Everything I see is made out of somebody's dream, and if I'm gonna be living in dreams they might as well be my own.

So right then and there I start making promises: I will wear wings at all hours of the night. I will laugh so loud the leaves fall all around me, I will walk with giant steps and swing my arms in enormous circles, I will take off my shoes when I come into the house and I will never, never leave my hopes to dry on the drainboard. I won't sleep in except when I do, I'll take walks in the woods and in the loud polluted city, I'll sing off pitch when I'm not alone. I will take off my masks and wear love unabashedly. I will keep making promises.

And I will not stop dreaming.